# THE ETERNAL SANDS: A JOURNEY THROUGH ANCIENT EGYPT'S CIVILIZATION

## J H W Williams

**Amazon**

ISBN: 9798391665632

# CONTENTS

# THE ALLURE OF ANCIENT EGYPT: A BRIEF OVERVIEW

By J. H. W. Williams

The timeless fascination with Ancient Egypt's rich history, culture, and mythology has captivated countless minds, including my own, for generations. As the author of this book, I, J. H. W. Williams, have been on a lifelong journey to uncover the secrets and delve into the mysteries of this remarkable civilization. Through my passion for Egyptology, I have been able to shed light on the stories of gods, pharaohs, and dynasties that have shaped the course of history and continue to inspire us today.

Ancient Egypt, a civilization that rose to prominence around 5,000 years ago, has left an indelible mark on the human story. The remnants of their magnificent monuments, such as the Great Pyramids of Giza, the Sphinx, and the temples of Luxor and Karnak, still stand as a testament to their extraordinary achievements. Beyond these awe-inspiring structures, Egypt has given us some of the most remarkable works of art, literature, and technological innovations that continue to captivate and influence modern society.

For centuries, the Nile River has been the lifeblood of Egypt, providing sustenance and a means of transportation for its people. The Nile's annual flooding brought fertile soil and water to the arid lands, allowing the Egyptians to develop a complex agricultural system and establish a centralised state that would flourish for millennia. The unique geographic isolation of Egypt, bordered by deserts to the east and west, and cataracts to the south, enabled the civilization to develop with minimal external influence, leading to a distinctive and unified culture.

The pantheon of Egyptian gods and goddesses, intricately woven into the fabric of their society, offers a profound insight into the Egyptian worldview. Gods such as Osiris, Isis, Horus, and Ra held sway over the forces of nature, the afterlife, and the cosmos. The pharaohs, considered divine rulers, were seen as the earthly embodiment of the gods, responsible for maintaining order and ensuring the prosperity of the land. The stories of their lives and reigns are intricately linked to the history of Ancient Egypt, and their legacies continue to inspire us today.

The history of Ancient Egypt is vast and complex, encompassing more than 30 dynasties and 3,000 years of history. From the Early Dynastic Period to the Greco-Roman Period, Egypt's story is one of triumphs and setbacks, innovation, and tradition. It is through the study of this great civilization that we can gain a better understanding of our shared human experience and the forces that have shaped the world in which we live.

This book, "The Eternal Sands: A Journey Through Ancient Egypt's Civilization," aims to provide a comprehensive and engaging exploration of this rich and diverse civilization. With 30 chapters spanning the major periods, dynasties, and cultural developments of Ancient Egypt, we will embark on a journey that uncovers the stories of gods, pharaohs, and the people who lived, loved, and died in this extraordinary land. Drawing on the latest archaeological discoveries and scholarly research, we will piece together a vivid picture of the ancient Egyptian world, highlighting its most remarkable achievements, enduring mysteries, and lasting legacy.

So, join me, J. H. W. Williams, as we set forth on a journey through time, exploring the eternal sands of Ancient Egypt and uncovering the fascinating tales of this incredible civilization. Together, we will delve into a world filled with wonder and intrigue, seeking to understand the forces that shaped the history of one of humanity's greatest and most enduring cultures

# CHAPTER 1: THE DAWN OF EGYPTIAN CIVILIZATION

The cradle of a remarkable civilization, Ancient Egypt has captured the imagination of scholars and enthusiasts alike for generations. The dawn of Egyptian civilization can be traced back to the Predynastic Period and the Early Dynastic Period, which laid the groundwork for the emergence of one of the most enduring and influential cultures in human history.

Predynastic Period: The Formation of a Nation

The story of Ancient Egypt begins around 6000 BCE with the Predynastic Period, a time when small agricultural communities dotted the Nile Valley. These early settlements were primarily focused on cultivating the fertile lands along the riverbanks, taking advantage of the Nile's life-giving resources. Over time, these communities began to interact, trade, and eventually merge, giving rise to the formation of a more complex society.

The Predynastic Period can be divided into several phases, including the Badarian, Amratian (or Naqada I), and the Gerzean (or Naqada II) cultures. The Badarian culture, which emerged around 4400 BCE, was characterised by small, semi-nomadic communities that engaged in agriculture and animal husbandry. The Amratian culture, which succeeded the Badarian around 4000 BCE, saw the establishment of larger, more permanent settlements and the introduction of pottery, decorated with intricate designs.

The Gerzean culture, emerging around 3500 BCE, was the most advanced phase of the Predynastic Period. This culture witnessed the development of a more sophisticated material culture, with an emphasis on craftsmanship and artistic expression. Advances in pottery, metallurgy, and stone-working marked this era, as well as the emergence of early hieroglyphic writing. Trade networks expanded, bringing valuable resources such as lapis lazuli, gold, and obsidian into Egypt. This period also saw the first inklings of social stratification and the establishment of powerful regional leaders who would eventually pave the way for the unification of Egypt.

Early Dynastic Period: The First Pharaohs

The Early Dynastic Period, which began around 3100 BCE, marked the birth of the world's first nation-state, as the Upper and Lower Egypt regions were united under a single ruler. This unification is often attributed to the legendary King Narmer, who is depicted on the famous Narmer Palette wearing both the White Crown of Upper Egypt and the Red Crown of Lower Egypt. With this historic unification, the age of the pharaohs began, and Egypt embarked on a journey that would shape the course of human history.

The Early Dynastic Period, spanning the First and Second Dynasties, was characterised by the establishment of a centralised administration, the development of hieroglyphic writing, and the construction of monumental structures that foreshadowed the grandiose architecture of later periods. The capital city during this era was Memphis, strategically located at the junction of Upper and Lower Egypt. The city would remain an important political and religious centre throughout Ancient Egypt's history.

Egypt's first pharaohs focused on consolidating their rule, expanding their territories, and establishing a divine kingship that would endure for millennia. Early pharaohs, such as Djoser and Khasekhemwy, undertook ambitious building projects, including the construction of elaborate tombs and mortuary complexes. These early tombs, known as mastabas, were precursors to the pyramids that would come to symbolise

Egypt's monumental legacy.

During the Early Dynastic Period, the religious beliefs and practices that would define Ancient Egypt began to take shape. The Egyptians believed in an intricate pantheon of gods and goddesses, each responsible for specific aspects of nature, the cosmos, and daily life. The pharaohs, considered divine rulers, were believed to be the earthly embodiment of the gods, maintaining the balance between the forces of chaos and order, and ensuring the prosperity and wellbeing of their subjects. This divine kingship would be a cornerstone of Egyptian civilization, with pharaohs ruling as god-kings for the next three millennia.

The Early Dynastic Period saw significant advancements in art, literature, and technology. Skilled artisans created intricate carvings, sculptures, and pottery, reflecting the natural world and the divine beings they revered. Early examples of hieroglyphic writing, such as the inscriptions found in tombs and on the Narmer Palette, indicate the beginnings of a complex system of record-keeping and communication. Technological innovations, such as the development of copper tools and advancements in agriculture, allowed the Egyptians to build a prosperous and stable society, which would serve as a foundation for the remarkable achievements of the Old Kingdom.

The end of the Early Dynastic Period is marked by the transition to the Old Kingdom, a time when Egypt would reach the zenith of its architectural and artistic accomplishments. The legacy of the Early Dynastic Period, however, should not be underestimated. The unification of Egypt, the establishment of a centralised government, the development of religious beliefs and practices, and the innovations in art and technology during this era laid the groundwork for the remarkable civilization that would captivate the world for generations to come.

In conclusion, the dawn of Egyptian civilization during the Predynastic and Early Dynastic Periods was a time of rapid development and growth, which laid the foundations for the extraordinary achievements that would follow. From small agricultural communities along the Nile, a complex and unified society emerged, driven by the vision and determination of its first pharaohs. These early rulers, such as Narmer, Djoser, and Khasekhemwy, set the stage for the grandiosity and splendour of the Old Kingdom, establishing a divine kingship that would endure for thousands of years.

In the chapters to come, we will explore the magnificent eras of Ancient Egypt, delving into the stories of the gods, pharaohs, and the people who built this remarkable civilization. From the towering pyramids of Giza to the mysterious tombs of the Valley of the Kings, we will uncover the secrets and marvels of a civilization that continues to captivate the hearts and minds of scholars and enthusiasts to this day. So join us as we embark on a journey through the eternal sands of Ancient Egypt, revealing the tales of triumph, tragedy, and timeless allure that have made this civilization an enduring testament to the indomitable human spirit.

# CHAPTER 2: THE NILE: THE LIFEBLOOD OF EGYPT

The Nile River, stretching over 4,000 miles through northeastern Africa, has long been recognized as the lifeblood of Egypt. This mighty river and its annual inundation have not only shaped the landscape but also the very fabric of Egyptian civilization. In this chapter, we will explore the vital role that the Nile played in the development and sustenance of Ancient Egypt, from the emergence of the first agricultural communities to the grandiosity of the pharaohs' reigns.

A River of Bounty: The Nile's Gifts to Egypt

Winding its way through the parched landscape of northeastern Africa, the Nile River is the longest river in the world. Originating from two main tributaries, the White Nile and the Blue Nile, the river traverses eleven countries before emptying into the Mediterranean Sea. It is in Egypt, however, that the Nile has left its most indelible mark, nurturing an ancient civilization that would stand as a testament to human ingenuity and perseverance.

The Nile's annual flooding, known as the inundation, was of paramount importance to the Ancient Egyptians. Each year, the floodwaters would recede, leaving behind a rich layer of fertile silt that transformed the arid land into a thriving agricultural haven. The inundation allowed the Egyptians to cultivate an array of crops, such as wheat, barley, flax, and papyrus, which were essential for their sustenance and economy. The river also provided an abundance of fish and waterfowl, supplementing the Egyptians' diet and contributing to their prosperity.

The inundation was so crucial to the survival of Ancient Egypt that it was deeply intertwined with their religious beliefs and mythology. The annual flood was seen as a manifestation of the tears of the goddess Isis, mourning for her slain husband, Osiris. The Egyptians believed that the god Hapi, the personification of the Nile, was responsible for the inundation and was dutifully worshipped and honoured to ensure the continuation of this life-giving event.

A Highway Through Time: The Nile as a Means of Transportation

Beyond its agricultural significance, the Nile River also served as a vital transportation network, connecting the various regions of Egypt and facilitating trade, communication, and the movement of people. The river's predictable and gentle currents allowed the Egyptians to develop sophisticated boats and ships, enabling them to traverse the Nile with ease.

The Nile was, in many ways, the ancient equivalent of a modern highway, with settlements, cities, and temples dotting its banks. The Egyptians relied heavily on the river for the transportation of goods, such as grain, stone, and luxury items, as well as for military and diplomatic expeditions. The Nile's importance as a means of transportation is evident in the many reliefs and inscriptions that depict grand processions of boats, laden with offerings and tribute for the gods and the pharaohs.

The river also played a crucial role in the construction of Egypt's most iconic monuments. The massive stone blocks used to build the pyramids, temples, and tombs were often quarried far from their final destination and transported along the Nile using wooden sleds and boats. This remarkable feat of engineering and logistics would not have been possible without the river's life-giving waters and its role as a vital transportation artery.

Water and Spirituality: The Nile in Religion and Ritual

The Nile's significance in Ancient Egyptian life extended beyond its practical contributions to agriculture and transportation.

The river was deeply embedded in the Egyptians' religious beliefs and practices, with many gods and goddesses associated with its life-giving waters. In addition to Hapi, the god of the inundation, the Egyptians revered the goddess Isis, whose tears were believed to cause the annual flood, and her husband, Osiristhe god of the underworld and rebirth, who was often associated with the fertile soil deposited by the Nile.

Temples and shrines dedicated to these deities were built along the riverbanks, and the Nile's waters played a central role in various religious rituals and ceremonies. The purification rites, essential to maintaining ritual purity, involved the use of Nile water, which was believed to possess healing and purifying properties. The river was also the setting for grand religious processions, such as the Beautiful Feast of Opet, during which the god Amun, his wife Mut, and their son Khonsu were paraded on sacred barques from the Karnak Temple to the Luxor Temple, symbolising the rejuvenation of the divine and earthly realms.

The Nile was also intimately connected to the concept of the afterlife in Ancient Egyptian beliefs. The river was seen as a reflection of the celestial Nile, which was thought to flow through the heavens, transporting the souls of the deceased to the afterlife. The journey to the afterlife was often depicted as a voyage along the Nile, guided by the sun god Ra, in his solar barque, and the deceased would be buried with models of boats and ships to ensure safe passage through the eternal realm.

The Enduring Legacy of the Nile

In conclusion, the Nile River was the lifeblood of Ancient Egypt, providing not only sustenance and transportation but also imbuing the civilization's religious beliefs and cultural practices with a deep reverence for the natural world. The river's annual inundation was a source of both wonder and relief for the Egyptians, who depended on its fertile silt and abundant resources to build a prosperous and stable society. The Nile's role as a highway through time facilitated trade, communication, and the construction of monumental structures that continue to captivate the world today.

The Nile's influence on Egyptian civilization cannot be overstated. It was a constant presence, shaping the lives of the people who lived along its banks and leaving an indelible mark on the history of humanity. The stories of the Nile and its role in the development of Ancient Egypt are a testament to the resilience and ingenuity of the human spirit, providing a window into the past and a source of inspiration for generations to come.

As we continue our journey through the eternal sands of Ancient Egypt, the Nile's enduring legacy will serve as a constant reminder of the vital role that nature and the environment play in shaping the course of human history. From the dawn of civilization to the zenith of the pharaohs' rule, the Nile River stands as a witness to the triumphs, setbacks, and the enduring allure of a civilization that has forever captured our collective imagination.

# CHAPTER 3: PREDYNASTIC PERIOD: THE FORMATION OF A NATION

In the vast expanse of human history, the Predynastic Period of Ancient Egypt occupies a unique and pivotal position. It was during this time that the foundations of a complex, unified civilization were laid, paving the way for the achievements and splendour that would come to define Egypt for millennia. In this chapter, we delve into the intricacies of the Predynastic Period, examining the social, cultural, and technological developments that transformed a series of disparate agricultural communities into the world's first nation-state.

A Tapestry of Cultures: The Predynastic Period in Context

The Predynastic Period, which began around 6000 BCE, witnessed the gradual evolution of small, semi-nomadic agricultural communities into larger, more complex societies. The Nile Valley, with its fertile soil and abundant resources, provided an ideal environment for the growth of these communities, which would eventually coalesce into the unified Egyptian civilization we know today.

The Predynastic Period can be broadly divided into several phases, each characterised by distinct cultural and technological innovations. These phases include the Badarian, Amratian (or Naqada I), and the Gerzean (or Naqada II) cultures, which laid the groundwork for the emergence of a more cohesive and sophisticated society.

The Badarian Culture: Early Beginnings (c. 4400 – 4000 BCE)

The Badarian culture marks the earliest phase of the Predynastic Period, characterised by small, semi-nomadic communities that practised agriculture and animal husbandry. These early settlements were primarily focused on cultivating the fertile lands along the Nile, taking advantage of the life-giving resources provided by the river.

Archaeological evidence from the Badarian period reveals the beginnings of a distinct material culture, characterised by the use of black-topped pottery, flint tools, and cosmetic palettes. The presence of simple, oval-shaped tombs suggests that the Badarians held rudimentary beliefs in the afterlife and buried their dead with modest grave goods.

The Amratian Culture: The Emergence of a Distinct Identity (c. 4000 – 3500 BCE)

The Amratian culture, which followed the Badarian, saw the establishment of larger, more permanent settlements, and the introduction of finely decorated pottery. The pottery from this period is adorned with intricate designs, often depicting animals and natural motifs, reflecting the growing artistic and cultural sophistication of these early Egyptians.

The Amratian period also marked the emergence of a distinct Egyptian identity, as regional leaders began to consolidate their power and assert their authority over surrounding communities. This process of political centralization laid the groundwork for the formation of a more complex society and the eventual unification of Egypt under a single ruler.

The Gerzean Culture: The Birth of a Complex Society (c. 3500 – 3200 BCE)

The Gerzean culture represents the most advanced phase of the Predynastic Period, witnessing the development of a more sophisticated material culture and social structure. Advances in pottery, metallurgy, and stone-working characterised this era, as well as the emergence of early hieroglyphic writing, which would become the hallmark of Ancient Egyptian civilization.

During the Gerzean period, trade networks expanded, bringing valuable resources such as lapis lazuli, gold, and obsidian into Egypt. This increased access to luxury goods and raw materials fueled the growth of a more stratified society, with regional leaders consolidating power and wealth. These leaders, often referred to as "proto-pharaohs," laid the foundation for the divine kingship that would define Egyptian civilization for thousands of years.

Archaeological evidence from the Gerzean period also reveals the development of more complex religious beliefs and practices. The construction of larger, more elaborate tombs and the presence of an increasing variety of grave goods indicate a growing concern with the afterlife and the desire to ensure a comfortable existence for the deceased. This period also saw the rise of cults dedicated to various deities, such as Hathor, the goddess of love and fertility, and Anubis, the god of mummification and the afterlife. These early religious practices would evolve and expand over time, eventually giving rise to the complex and intricate belief system that characterised Ancient Egyptian religion.

The Road to Unification: The Advent of Dynastic Egypt (c. 3200 – 3000 BCE)

The culmination of the Predynastic Period came with the unification of Upper and Lower Egypt under a single ruler, an event that marked the beginning of Egypt's First Dynasty and the advent of the Old Kingdom. While the precise details of this unification remain shrouded in myth and legend, it is generally attributed to the ruler Narmer, who is depicted on the famous Narmer Palette wearing the crowns of both Upper and Lower Egypt.

The unification of Egypt represented a significant turning point in the nation's history, as the disparate cultures of the Nile Valley came together to form a cohesive and powerful civilization. This event laid the groundwork for the emergence of the divine kingship that would come to define Ancient Egyptian society, as well as the remarkable achievements in art, architecture, and literature that would follow.

In conclusion, the Predynastic Period of Ancient Egypt was a time of remarkable growth and transformation, as the small agricultural communities of the Nile Valley evolved into a complex, unified civilization. This period witnessed the development of a distinct Egyptian identity, characterised by advances in art, technology, and social structure. The emergence of regional leaders and the eventual unification of Egypt under a single ruler set the stage for the grandeur and splendour of the pharaohs' reigns, as well as the remarkable achievements that would come to define Ancient Egyptian civilization.

As we continue our journey through the sands of time, the lessons and legacies of the Predynastic Period serve as a testament to the indomitable human spirit and the power of cultural exchange, innovation, and adaptation. From the humble beginnings of the Badarian culture to the awe-inspiring achievements of the Gerzean society, the story of the Predynastic Period is a testament to the potential of humanity to overcome adversity and forge a brighter future, even in the harshest of environments.

[1]

The Early Dynastic Period, spanning the First and Second Dynasties of Ancient Egypt (c. 3100 – 2686 BCE), was a crucial era in the nation's history. Following the unification of Upper and Lower Egypt under a single ruler, this period witnessed the emergence of the divine kingship that would come to define Egyptian society for millennia. In this chapter, we explore the reigns of the first pharaohs, their monumental achievements, and the social and cultural developments that marked the dawn of Dynastic Egypt.

A New Era of Leadership: The Advent of the Pharaoh

With the unification of Egypt under Narmer, the stage was set for the development of a new form of leadership – the divine kingship embodied by the pharaoh. The pharaohs of the Early Dynastic Period were seen as intermediaries between the gods and their subjects, responsible for maintaining the cosmic order known as Ma'at. This divine mandate placed the pharaoh at the centre of Egyptian society, both as a political leader and a religious figure.

The pharaohs of the Early Dynastic Period, including Narmer, Aha, Djer, and Den, consolidated their power by establishing a centralized administration, with regional governors known as nomarchs overseeing the various provinces, or nomes, of Egypt. This system of governance allowed the pharaohs to exert control over the vast Egyptian territories and maintain the stability and prosperity of their kingdom.

Monumental Achievements: The First Royal Tombs and the Step Pyramid

The Early Dynastic Period saw the construction of some of Egypt's most iconic and enduring monuments. The pharaohs of the First Dynasty built elaborate tombs for themselves at Abydos, a sacred site dedicated to the god Osiris, reflecting their concern for the afterlife and their desire to ensure a favorable journey to the eternal realm.

One of the most notable tombs from this period is that of Pharaoh Djer, which featured a large, rectangular burial chamber and a series of subsidiary tombs for his royal court. This grandiose burial complex set the standard for royal tombs in subsequent dynasties and paved the way for the monumental achievements of the Old Kingdom, such as the Step Pyramid of Djoser.

The Step Pyramid, constructed during the reign of Pharaoh

Djoser of the Third Dynasty, represented a significant innovation in Egyptian architecture and engineering. Designed by the legendary architect Imhotep, the Step Pyramid was the first large-scale stone structure in the world, consisting of six stepped layers that rose to a height of 62 meters. This magnificent monument not only reflected the pharaoh's divine status but also signaled the growing sophistication of Egyptian society and its ability to harness the resources and labor required for such monumental undertakings.

Cultural and Artistic Developments: The Birth of a Unique Identity

The Early Dynastic Period was also marked by significant cultural and artistic developments that would come to define Ancient Egyptian civilization. The period saw the refinement of hieroglyphic writing, which became the primary means of communication and record-keeping for the Egyptian state. The development of hieroglyphs allowed for the creation of elaborate inscriptions on monuments, temples, and tombs, preserving the stories and achievements of the pharaohs for posterity.

Artistic expression during the Early Dynastic Period was characterized by a distinctive style that emphasized symmetry, balance, and a sense of order. This style is evident in the exquisite craftsmanship of the Narmer Palette, which commemorates the unification of Egypt, as well as the funerary stelae and statues that adorned the tombs of the First Dynasty pharaohs. These artistic achievements reflect the growing cultural sophistication of Egyptian society and the emergence of a unique artistic identity that would endure for thousands of years.

In addition to artistic advancements, the Early Dynastic Period saw the development of a rich religious tradition that permeated all aspects of Egyptian life. The pantheon of gods and goddesses, which included deities such as Ra, Isis, Osiris, and Anubis, continued to evolve and expand, reflecting the complex belief system that underpinned Egyptian society. Temples dedicated to these deities were constructed throughout Egypt, serving as centers of worship and community life.

Daily Life and Social Structure in the Early Dynastic Period

The social structure of the Early Dynastic Period was highly stratified, with the pharaoh and his royal family occupying the pinnacle of society. Below the royal family were the nobles, priests, and high-ranking officials who managed the affairs of the kingdom on behalf of the pharaoh. At the bottom of the social hierarchy were the farmers, laborers, and slaves who performed the manual labor necessary to sustain the economy and support the construction of monumental projects.

Despite the rigid social hierarchy, daily life in the Early Dynastic Period was marked by a degree of stability and prosperity, as the centralized administration and efficient management of resources ensured that the basic needs of the population were met. Agriculture formed the backbone of the Egyptian economy, with farmers cultivating the fertile lands along the Nile and producing abundant harvests of grain, fruits, and vegetables.

Trade also played a significant role in the Early Dynastic Period, with Egypt establishing trade networks with neighboring regions such as Nubia, the Levant, and Mesopotamia. These trade relationships facilitated the exchange of goods and ideas, enriching Egyptian society and contributing to its cultural and technological development.

The Legacy of the Early Dynastic Period

The Early Dynastic Period marked the dawn of a new era in human history, as the disparate cultures of the Nile Valley came together to form a complex, powerful civilization that would endure for millennia. The reigns of the first pharaohs, their monumental achievements, and the social and cultural developments that characterized this period laid the foundation for the grandeur and splendor of Ancient Egypt.

As we continue our journey through the sands of time, the legacies of the Early Dynastic Period stand as a testament to the indomitable human spirit and the power of collective endeavor. From the unification of Egypt under Narmer to the construction of the world's first large-scale stone structure, the story of the Early Dynastic Period is a celebration of human ingenuity, resilience, and the enduring allure of a civilization that has forever captured our collective imagination.

# CHAPTER 4: THE OLD KINGDOM - THE AGE OF THE PYRAMIDS

The Old Kingdom (c. 2686 – 2181 BCE) stands as one of the most remarkable periods in Ancient Egyptian history, an era marked by grandiose achievements in art, architecture, and political organization. Often referred to as the "Age of the Pyramids," the Old Kingdom witnessed the construction of the iconic pyramids of Giza, which have endured as symbols of human ingenuity and the indomitable spirit of the Egyptian civilization. In this part, we delve into the wonders and legacies of the Old Kingdom, exploring the reigns of its greatest pharaohs, the extraordinary architectural feats that defined the era, and the cultural and social developments that shaped the lives of its people.

# CHAPTER 5: THE AGE OF PYRAMIDS: DYNASTIES 3-6

The Age of Pyramids, spanning the Third to the Sixth Dynasties of the Old Kingdom, stands as a testament to the grandeur and sophistication of Ancient Egyptian civilization. This period, characterized by remarkable achievements in architecture, art, and political organization, is defined by the construction of the iconic pyramids that continue to captivate the world. In this chapter, we explore the history and accomplishments of the Third to Sixth Dynasties, examining the reigns of the greatest pharaohs, the extraordinary architectural feats of the time, and the cultural and social developments that shaped this remarkable era.

The Third Dynasty: Foundations of the Age of Pyramids

The Third Dynasty (c. 2686 – 2613 BCE) marked the beginning of the Old Kingdom and laid the groundwork for the monumental achievements that would come to define the Age of Pyramids. Under the rule of Pharaoh Djoser, Egypt experienced a period of stability and prosperity, as advances in art, architecture, and technology contributed to the growing sophistication of Egyptian society. The reign of Djoser is particularly significant due to the construction of the Step Pyramid, the world's first large-scale stone structure. Designed by the legendary architect Imhotep, the Step Pyramid not only symbolized Djoser's divine status but also demonstrated the ability of the Egyptian state to marshal the resources and labor required for such ambitious undertakings.

The Fourth Dynasty: The Golden Age of the Pyramids

The Fourth Dynasty (c. 2613 – 2494 BCE) is often considered the zenith of the Old Kingdom, an era marked by the construction of the iconic pyramids of Giza, the most enduring symbols of Ancient Egyptian civilization. The reigns of Pharaohs Khufu, Khafre, and Menkaure, who were responsible for the construction of the Great Pyramid, the Pyramid of Khafre, and the Pyramid of Menkaure, respectively, were characterized by remarkable achievements in engineering, art, and literature.

The Great Pyramid of Giza, built by Pharaoh Khufu, remains one of the most impressive feats of human engineering. As the largest of the three pyramids, it was constructed using an estimated 2.3 million limestone blocks, each weighing an average of 2.5 tons. The precision and ingenuity required to build such a colossal monument is a testament to the skill and determination of the architects, engineers, and laborers of the Fourth Dynasty.

Pharaoh Khafre, Khufu's successor, is best known for the construction of the Pyramid of Khafre and the Great Sphinx, a massive limestone statue with the body of a lion and the head of a human, believed to represent Khafre himself. The Great Sphinx remains one of the most iconic and enigmatic monuments of Ancient Egypt, symbolizing the power and wisdom of the pharaoh.

Pharaoh Menkaure, the last of the great pyramid builders, commissioned the construction of the smallest of the three pyramids of Giza, the Pyramid of Menkaure. Though smaller in scale, Menkaure's pyramid is notable for its high-quality construction and the use of granite casing stones, which give the monument a distinctive appearance.

The Fifth and Sixth Dynasties: Decline and Transformation

The Fifth and Sixth Dynasties (c. 2494 – 2181 BCE) marked a period of decline and transformation for the Old Kingdom. The construction of colossal pyramids gradually ceased, and the focus shifted to smaller, more modest tombs and mortuary complexes. This period also witnessed the decentralisation of power, as regional governors, or nomarches, began to assert greater autonomy, ultimately contributing to the fragmentation of the Egyptian state.

Despite the challenges of this period, the Fifth and Sixth Dynasties were marked by significant cultural and intellectual achievements. The emergence of the "Sun Cult," which revolved around the worship of the sun god Ra, led to the construction of sun temples, such as the one built by Pharaoh Userkaf, the founder of the Fifth Dynasty. These temples featured obelisks and other architectural elements that captured the essence of solar worship, reflecting the evolving religious beliefs of the time.

The Pyramid Texts, a collection of religious and funerary inscriptions, were first developed during the Fifth and Sixth Dynasties. These texts, carved on the walls of the pyramids and tombs of the pharaohs, provide valuable insight into the religious beliefs, rituals, and practices of the Old Kingdom, as well as the daily lives and concerns of its people.

One of the most significant cultural achievements of the Fifth and Sixth Dynasties was the development of a vibrant literary tradition. The "Autobiography of Weni," an inscription on the tomb of a high-ranking official named Weni, is an example of the personal narratives that flourished during this period. These autobiographical inscriptions offer a unique perspective on the lives and experiences of individuals in Ancient Egyptian society, providing an intimate glimpse into their thoughts, emotions, and aspirations.

In addition to literature, art and craftsmanship continued to thrive during the Fifth and Sixth Dynasties. The exquisite reliefs and sculptures that adorned the tombs of the period are evidence of the enduring artistic skill and creativity of the Ancient Egyptians, even as their civilization faced mounting challenges.

Conclusion: The Enduring Legacy of the Age of Pyramids

The Age of Pyramids, spanning the Third to Sixth Dynasties of the Old Kingdom, remains one of the most remarkable periods in human history. The construction of the iconic pyramids and the development of a sophisticated civilization marked by advances in art, architecture, and political organisation continue to captivate and inspire us today.

As we reflect on the accomplishments of the Age of Pyramids, we are reminded of the indomitable spirit and ingenuity of the Ancient Egyptians, who built monumental structures and forged a unique cultural identity that has left an indelible mark on the sands of time. The legacies of the pharaohs, their awe-inspiring architectural feats, and the vibrant culture that blossomed during this era continue to resonate, providing a glimpse into the rich tapestry of human history and the enduring allure of a civilization that has forever captured our collective imagination.

# CHAPTER 6: THE GREAT PYRAMID OF GIZA: A LASTING WONDER

The Great Pyramid of Giza stands as a timeless testament to the ingenuity, ambition, and perseverance of the Ancient Egyptians. As one of the Seven Wonders of the Ancient World and the last remaining wonder still standing, this awe-inspiring monument continues to captivate and inspire us millennia after its construction. In this chapter, we delve into the history, design, and construction of the Great Pyramid, exploring its enduring significance and the reasons behind its lasting fascination.

The Vision and Purpose of the Great Pyramid

Built during the Fourth Dynasty (c. 2613 – 2494 BCE) under the rule of Pharaoh Khufu, the Great Pyramid was conceived as the ultimate resting place for the pharaoh, a grandiose monument that would not only ensure his eternal legacy but also demonstrate the power and might of the Egyptian state. The construction of the Great Pyramid was an unparalleled feat of engineering and logistics, requiring the mobilisation of vast resources, labour, and technical expertise.

The precise purpose of the Great Pyramid has been a subject of debate and speculation for centuries. While it is generally accepted that the pyramid served as a tomb for Khufu, some scholars have proposed alternative theories, suggesting that it might have been a colossal astronomical observatory, a representation of sacred geometry, or even a means to facilitate the pharaoh's ascension to the stars. Regardless of its intended purpose, the Great Pyramid remains an enduring symbol of the creative and spiritual aspirations of the Ancient Egyptians.

The Design and Construction of the Great Pyramid

The Great Pyramid of Giza is a marvel of engineering and architectural design, reflecting the advanced knowledge and skill of its builders. It stands approximately 481 feet (146.5 metres) tall, originally measuring 480.6 feet (146.6 metres) before the erosion of its outer casing stones. The pyramid was constructed using an estimated 2.3 million limestone blocks, each weighing an average of 2.5 tons, with some of the larger granite blocks weighing as much as 80 tons.

The precise methods employed in the construction of the Great Pyramid remain a subject of debate among scholars and engineers. Several theories have been proposed, ranging from the use of ramps, levers, and counterweights to more speculative ideas involving the harnessing of sound or electromagnetic energy. While the exact techniques used by the Ancient Egyptians to build the pyramid are still a mystery, the monument stands as a testament to their remarkable ingenuity and determination.

One of the most intriguing aspects of the Great Pyramid is the precision with which it was built. The pyramid is aligned almost perfectly with the cardinal points of the compass, with an error margin of less than one degree. The accuracy of this alignment suggests that the Ancient Egyptians had advanced knowledge of astronomy and mathematics, as well as a deep understanding of the spiritual significance of the cosmos.

The Enduring Fascination with the Great Pyramid

The Great Pyramid of Giza has captivated the imagination of countless generations, inspiring a sense of wonder and awe that transcends time and culture. As the last remaining wonder of the ancient world, the pyramid has been a source of fascination for historians, archaeologists, and tourists alike, drawing millions of visitors to its imposing base each year.

The lasting allure of the Great Pyramid can be attributed to its sheer scale, the precision of its construction, and the enigmatic nature of its purpose. For many, the pyramid represents the pinnacle of human achievement, a testament to the indomitable spirit and creativity of a civilization that flourished millennia ago. Its enduring mystery and grandeur continue to spark curiosity and inspire awe, inviting us to ponder the ingenuity and aspirations of the Ancient Egyptians.

In conclusion, the Great Pyramid of Giza is a lasting wonder that serves as a tangible connection to the ancient world and a powerful reminder of the extraordinary capabilities of human civilization. Its timeless appeal lies in the intricate combination of architectural genius, astronomical precision, and the enigmatic purpose that has drawn scholars and enthusiasts from around the world to study and admire its magnificence.

The Great Pyramid also offers invaluable insights into the religious beliefs, cultural practices, and technological prowess of the Ancient Egyptians. As we continue to explore and uncover the secrets of this remarkable monument, we are reminded of the importance of preserving and celebrating our shared cultural heritage, which transcends geographical boundaries and connects us through the annals of human history.

As we gaze upon the colossal structure that has withstood the ravages of time, we are humbled by the achievements of a civilization that existed thousands of years ago. The Great Pyramid of Giza stands as a lasting testament to the indomitable spirit of human ingenuity, the power of collective effort, and the eternal quest for knowledge and understanding that drives our species forward.

In the shadow of the Great Pyramid, we find a source of inspiration and a tangible connection to the past, inviting us to reflect on our own place in the grand tapestry of human history. As we contemplate the legacy of the Ancient Egyptians and the enduring wonder of the Great Pyramid, we are reminded of our own capacity for greatness and the boundless potential of human endeavour.

# CHAPTER 7: GODS AND GODDESSES OF THE OLD KINGDOM

The Old Kingdom of Ancient Egypt was a period marked by remarkable achievements in architecture, art, and political organisation, as well as the development of a rich and complex religious tradition. Central to the spiritual life of the Old Kingdom were the gods and goddesses who played vital roles in the creation of the universe, the maintenance of cosmic order, and the daily lives of the Egyptian people. In this chapter, we explore the fascinating pantheon of gods and goddesses of the Old Kingdom, examining their roles, attributes, and the various rituals and practices associated with their worship.

Atum: The Creator God

At the heart of Egyptian cosmology was the belief in a divine creator responsible for the emergence of the universe from the primordial waters of chaos. Atum, one of the earliest and most important creator gods, was believed to have emerged from the waters of Nun and, through an act of divine self-generation, gave birth to the first divine couple, Shu and Tefnut. As the progenitor of the gods and the embodiment of the creative force, Atum was revered as the source of life and the ultimate divine authority.

Ra: The Sun God

One of the most important and widely worshipped deities of the Old Kingdom was Ra, the sun god. As the embodiment of the sun, Ra was believed to sail across the sky each day in a solar barque, bringing light and life to the world. Each night, he would descend into the underworld, where he would battle the forces of chaos and darkness, only to be reborn each morning at dawn. The daily journey of Ra symbolised the perpetual struggle between order and chaos, a central theme in Egyptian religion and cosmology.

Ra was also considered the divine ruler of the gods and the patron of the pharaohs. The pharaohs of the Old Kingdom were believed to be the earthly manifestations of Ra, their rule a reflection of the divine order established by the sun god himself.

Osiris: God of the Afterlife

The concept of the afterlife played a critical role in the religious beliefs and practices of the Old Kingdom, with the god Osiris reigning supreme as the lord of the dead. Osiris was associated with the Nile, agriculture, and the cycle of life, death, and rebirth. As the god of the afterlife, Osiris was responsible for the judgement of the dead and the ultimate determination of their fate in the afterlife.

According to Egyptian mythology, Osiris was murdered by his brother Set, who covered his throne. Osiris' wife, Isis, collected his dismembered body and used her magical powers to bring him back to life, allowing Osiris to become the ruler of the afterlife and a symbol of resurrection and eternal life.

Isis: The Mother Goddess

Isis, the wife of Osiris, was a multifaceted goddess associated with motherhood, fertility, magic, and healing. As the mother of Horus, the sky god and the divine protector of the pharaohs, Isis played a pivotal role in the divine royal lineage and the mythological narrative of the eternal struggle between good and evil. As a powerful magician and healer, Isis was also invoked for her ability to protect and heal the living, making her a beloved and widely worshipped deity.

Ptah: The Patron of Craftsmen

Ptah was the god of craftsmen and the patron of arts and architecture. As the divine creator of the physical world, Ptah was believed to have fashioned the universe through his thoughts and words. His association with craftsmanship made him a central figure in the construction and maintenance of temples, statues, and other sacred structures, as well as the production of sacred objects and ritual paraphernalia Divine Tapestry of the Old Kingdom

The gods and goddesses of the Old Kingdom formed a complex and interconnected web of divine relationships, embodying the various forces of nature, aspects of human experience, and the fundamental principles of Egyptian society. They played a crucial role in the daily lives of the Egyptian people, providing guidance, protection, and a sense of order and meaning to the world around them.

The worship of these deities involved a range of rituals and ceremonies, from the daily offerings made in the temples to the elaborate festivals that marked the passage of time and the changing of the seasons. The gods and goddesses were also intimately connected to the pharaohs, who were considered their earthly representatives and divine intermediaries.

The pantheon of gods and goddesses in the Old Kingdom reflected the rich and diverse religious landscape of Ancient Egypt, a testament to the profound spirituality and vivid imagination of its people. As we delve deeper into the stories and myths surrounding these divine beings, we gain a greater appreciation for the cultural richness and complexity of the Ancient Egyptian civilization and the profound spiritual legacy it has left behind.

The gods and goddesses of the Old Kingdom continue to captivate and inspire us today, their timeless tales and enduring symbols offering a fascinating window into the beliefs, values, and aspirations of a civilization that flourished thousands of years ago. As we continue to explore the divine tapestry of the Old Kingdom, we are reminded of the universal themes and timeless truths that bind us together as human beings, transcending the boundaries of time and space to reveal the shared heritage of our collective past.

# CHAPTER 8: THE OLD KINGDOM'S ART AND ARCHITECTURE

The Old Kingdom of Ancient Egypt was a period of remarkable artistic and architectural achievements, leaving behind a rich and enduring legacy that continues to captivate and inspire us today. The art and architecture of the Old Kingdom reflect the diverse cultural, religious, and political aspects of Egyptian society, providing a unique glimpse into the values, beliefs, and aspirations of this remarkable civilization. In this chapter, we delve into the various facets of Old Kingdom art and architecture, exploring the techniques, styles, and themes that defined this golden age of creativity and innovation.

The Art of the Old Kingdom

The art of the Old Kingdom was characterised by a sense of order, balance, and harmony, reflecting the underlying principles of Egyptian society and cosmology. Artists adhered to a strict set of rules and conventions that governed the proportions, colours, and compositions of their works, ensuring that their creations maintained a consistent visual language and a sense of continuity across time and space.

One of the most distinctive features of Old Kingdom art was its emphasis on idealisation and perfection. Artists sought to portray their subjects, whether human or divine, in an idealised and timeless manner, highlighting their beauty, power, and nobility while downplaying any imperfections or signs of age. This idealisation can be seen in the numerous statues, reliefs, and paintings that adorned the temples, tombs, and palaces of the Old Kingdom, their elegant forms and serene expressions conveying a sense of eternal grace and tranquillity.

Old Kingdom art also placed a strong emphasis on narrative

and symbolism, with artists using visual storytelling to convey complex religious, mythological, and historical themes. Scenes from daily life, such as hunting, farming, and craftsmanship, were depicted alongside grandiose depictions of religious rituals and divine beings, creating a rich and diverse visual tapestry that captured the essence of Egyptian culture and spirituality.

The Architecture of the Old Kingdom

The architecture of the Old Kingdom was characterised by monumental scale, technical prowess, and a deep sense of symbolism, with builders and architects pushing the boundaries of possibility in their quest to create enduring monuments to the gods, pharaohs, and the Egyptian state.

The most iconic architectural achievements of the Old Kingdom were, undoubtedly, the pyramids, colossal structures that served as the eternal resting places for the pharaohs and their queens. The construction of the pyramids represented the culmination of centuries of architectural and engineering experimentation, with builders developing innovative techniques and materials to create structures that would stand the test of time.

The Great Pyramid of Giza, built for Pharaoh Khufu during the Fourth Dynasty, stands as the most famous and enduring monument of the Old Kingdom. As we have discussed in Chapter 6, the Great Pyramid was an unparalleled feat of engineering and logistics, a testament to the ingenuity, ambition, and perseverance of the Ancient Egyptians.

In addition to the pyramids, the Old Kingdom was also marked by the construction of numerous temples, tombs, and palaces, each designed to serve a specific religious, funerary, or administrative function. These structures were adorned with exquisite reliefs, sculptures, and paintings, their intricate decorations serving both a decorative and a didactic purpose, as they were intended to convey important religious and moral messages to their viewers.

The Enduring Legacy of Old Kingdom Art and Architecture

The art and architecture of the Old Kingdom stand as a testament to the creativity, skill, and vision of the Ancient Egyptians, their timeless beauty and grandeur reflecting the values, beliefs, and aspirations of a civilization that has left an indelible mark on the sands of time.

As we continue to explore and appreciate the artistic and architectural achievements of the Old Kingdom, we are reminded of the importance of preserving and celebrating our shared cultural heritage, which serves as a bridge between the past and the present, allowing us to better understand our own history and the diverse human experiences that have shaped the world we live in today.

The Old Kingdom's art and architecture not only provide us with a fascinating glimpse into the lives and minds of the people who created them but also continue to inspire and influence contemporary artists, architects, and designers. From the pyramids' geometric precision and awe-inspiring scale to the refined beauty of the statues and reliefs, these ancient masterpieces have left a lasting impression on the creative endeavours of subsequent generations.

By studying and celebrating the achievements of the Old Kingdom, we are able to gain valuable insights into the power of art and architecture to transcend time, space, and cultural boundaries, serving as a unifying force that brings people together in a shared appreciation of beauty, innovation, and the human spirit.

In conclusion, the Old Kingdom's art and architecture represent a pinnacle of human creativity and ingenuity, a golden age of artistic expression and architectural innovation that has left an enduring and inspiring legacy for all who come after. As we continue to delve into the mysteries of the past and uncover the secrets of this remarkable civilization, we are constantly reminded of the profound impact that art and architecture have on our collective consciousness, shaping our understanding of ourselves, our history, and our place in the cosmos.

# CHAPTER 9: THE FIRST INTERMEDIATE PERIOD: A TIME OF TURMOIL

The First Intermediate Period (c. 2181-2055 BCE) marks a tumultuous time in Ancient Egypt's history. Following the collapse of the Old Kingdom, this era was characterised by political instability, fragmented rule, and social upheaval. Despite the challenges of this period, it laid the groundwork for the eventual reunification of Egypt under the Middle Kingdom. In this chapter, we will delve into the causes and consequences of the First Intermediate Period, shedding light on the resilience and adaptability of the Ancient Egyptians in the face of adversity.

The Fall of the Old Kingdom

The Old Kingdom's decline was a result of multiple factors, both internal and external. Economic troubles, coupled with a series of low Nile floods, led to widespread famine and social unrest. The power of the pharaohs diminished as local governors, known as nomarchs, gained more autonomy and influence, weakening the central government's authority.

These issues were further exacerbated by a succession crisis in the Sixth Dynasty, as several short-lived and relatively ineffective pharaohs struggled to maintain order. The Old Kingdom ultimately crumbled under the weight of these challenges, paving the way for the First Intermediate Period.

Political Fragmentation and Decentralization

The First Intermediate Period saw the fragmentation of Egypt into several smaller, competing factions. Nomarchs, who had gradually accumulated power during the later years of the Old

Kingdom, declared themselves rulers of their respective regions, contributing to the decentralisation of authority.

During this time, Egypt was divided primarily between the northern kingdom, based in Herakleopolis, and the southern kingdom, centred in Thebes. These two power centres vied for supremacy, leading to a series of military conflicts and shifting alliances. This unstable political landscape stood in stark contrast to the unified rule that characterised the Old Kingdom.

Social Upheaval and Cultural Changes

The First Intermediate Period was marked by significant social and cultural transformations. The decline of the centralised government resulted in a shift of power from the pharaohs and their elite officials to the nomarchs and other regional leaders. This decentralisation led to a more egalitarian society, with increased opportunities for social mobility and a greater emphasis on individual achievements.

This period also saw a flourishing of regional artistic styles and a diversification of subjects in Egyptian art. No longer confined to the strict conventions of the Old Kingdom, artists began to experiment with new forms and themes, reflecting the realities of daily life and the concerns of the common people. The social and cultural changes of the First Intermediate Period would continue to influence Egyptian society and art even after the reunification of the kingdom.

The Path to Reunification

The path to reunification was initiated by the Theban rulers of the Eleventh Dynasty, who sought to reestablish a centralised government and restore order to Egypt. Pharaoh Mentuhotep II (c. 2061-2010 BCE) is credited with successfully reunifying the country after defeating the Herakleopolitan rulers in a series of military campaigns.

Mentuhotep II's reign marked the beginning of the Middle

Kingdom and a return to stability, prosperity, and centralised rule. The First Intermediate Period, however, left a lasting impact on Egyptian society, politics, and culture, shaping the course of the nation's history for centuries to come.

The First Intermediate Period was a time of turmoil and transformation, a period of fragmentation and strife that ultimately led to the reunification of Egypt under the Middle Kingdom. Despite the challenges of this era, the Ancient Egyptians demonstrated remarkable resilience and adaptability, navigating the complexities of a rapidly changing world and laying the groundwork for a new age of prosperity and stability. The lessons of the First Intermediate Period serve as a testament to the enduring spirit and resourcefulness of the Ancient Egyptians, reminding us of the importance of perseverance and adaptability in the face of adversity.

During this tumultuous time, the Ancient Egyptians were forced to adapt to new political, social, and economic realities, as they grappled with the consequences of the Old Kingdom's decline. This period of upheaval and uncertainty brought about significant changes in Egyptian society, as power structures shifted and new opportunities for social mobility emerged. This more egalitarian society provided a foundation for the Middle Kingdom, which would build upon the lessons learned during the First Intermediate Period to create a more stable and prosperous nation.

The cultural and artistic developments of the First Intermediate Period were similarly significant, as artists broke free from the constraints of Old Kingdom conventions to explore new forms, styles, and themes. This artistic renaissance reflected the broader changes taking place in Egyptian society, capturing the spirit of innovation and resilience that defined this era.

In the end, the First Intermediate Period, though fraught with challenges, proved to be a crucible for change, shaping the course of Egyptian history and leaving an indelible mark on the nation's cultural, political, and social landscape. As we continue our journey through the history of Ancient Egypt, we are reminded of the importance of learning from the past, embracing change, and facing adversity with courage and determination, as the Ancient Egyptians did during this transformative period in their history.

# CHAPTER 10: THE MIDDLE KINGDOM: A PERIOD OF REUNIFICATION

The Middle Kingdom (c. 2055-1650 BCE) marked a resurgence of Egyptian power and cultural achievement following the turbulent First Intermediate Period. It was an era of reunification, prosperity, and increased international influence, laying the foundation for Egypt's subsequent imperial expansion during the New Kingdom. In this chapter, we will explore the key events, developments, and figures that characterised the Middle Kingdom, delving into the political, social, and cultural aspects of this dynamic period in Egyptian history.

The Eleventh Dynasty: Reunifying Egypt

As previously mentioned, the reunification of Egypt was initiated by the Theban rulers of the Eleventh Dynasty. Pharaoh Mentuhotep II (c. 2061-2010 BCE) played a pivotal role in this process, launching a series of military campaigns against the northern Herakleopolitan kingdom, which eventually led to its subjugation. Mentuhotep II's reign marked the beginning of the Middle Kingdom and heralded a new era of centralised rule and national unity.

The Twelfth Dynasty: Egypt's Golden Age

The Twelfth Dynasty (c. 1976-1793 BCE) is often regarded as the pinnacle of the Middle Kingdom, a time of unprecedented prosperity, stability, and cultural achievement. The dynasty was founded by Amenemhat I, who was possibly a vizier during the latter years of the Eleventh Dynasty, and he established a new capital at Itjtawy, located in the Faiyum region. This move further solidified the reunification of Egypt and centralised power.

Several notable pharaohs ruled during the Twelfth Dynasty, including Senusret I (c. 1956-1911 BCE), Senusret III (c. 1878-1860 BCE), and Amenemhat III (c. 1860-1815 BCE). Under their leadership, Egypt expanded its borders, built impressive monuments, and fostered an environment in which art, literature, and architecture flourished.

International Relations and Expansion

The Middle Kingdom saw a significant increase in Egypt's international influence, as the pharaohs established diplomatic ties and trade networks with neighbouring regions. Egypt expanded its reach into Nubia, Sinai, and the Levant, establishing a series of fortresses and trading posts to protect and maintain its interests.

The conquest of Lower Nubia was a key strategic objective for the Twelfth Dynasty pharaohs, who sought to control this resource-rich region and its lucrative trade routes. Under the reign of Senusret III, Egypt established a firm grip on Lower Nubia, integrating it into the Egyptian state and exploiting its wealth of gold, ivory, and other valuable commodities.

Art, Literature, and Religion in the Middle Kingdom

The Middle Kingdom was a period of profound artistic and literary innovation, as the cultural and social changes of the First Intermediate Period continued to shape Egypt's creative landscape. Artistic styles became more naturalistic and expressive, reflecting the concerns and aspirations of the common people as well as the elite. Monumental sculptures, such as the colossal statues of Senusret III, exemplify the skill and artistry of Middle Kingdom craftsmen.

Literature, too, thrived during this period, with the creation of various genres, including wisdom literature, poetry, and narrative tales. Works such as "The Tale of Sinuhe" and "The Instruction of Amenemhat" provide valuable insights into the intellectual and cultural life of the Middle Kingdom, revealing the concerns, values, and beliefs that shaped Egyptian society during this time.

Religion played a central role in the lives of the Ancient Egyptians, and the Middle Kingdom was no exception. The cult of Osiris, the god of the afterlife , grew in prominence during this period, as the concept of personal salvation and an afterlife accessible to all became more widespread. This shift in religious beliefs is reflected in the elaborate funerary practices and the construction of elaborate tombs for both royalty and the upper classes.

Architecture in the Middle Kingdom

The Middle Kingdom saw a resurgence of monumental architecture, as pharaohs and nobles sought to leave a lasting legacy through the construction of temples, tombs, and other grand structures. While pyramids remained the preferred burial monuments for the pharaohs, the designs of the Middle Kingdom pyramids differed from those of the Old Kingdom. The most famous Middle Kingdom pyramids are those of Amenemhat I, Senusret I, and Amenemhat III, located at Dahshur and Hawara.

In addition to pyramids, the Middle Kingdom also witnessed the construction of vast temple complexes, such as the Temple of Karnak in Thebes, which was expanded and embellished by various pharaohs throughout the Middle Kingdom and beyond. These temples served as centres of religious worship and were adorned with intricate reliefs, statues, and inscriptions that showcased the artistic and architectural prowess of the period.

The Decline of the Middle Kingdom

The Middle Kingdom's decline began during the later years of the Thirteenth Dynasty (c. 1793-1650 BCE), as the central government once again weakened and the power of the provincial nomarchs grew. The Egyptian state began to fragment, with competing factions vying for control.

The final blow to the Middle Kingdom came with the invasion of the Hyksos, a group of Asiatic people who seized control of the northern part of Egypt, establishing the Fifteenth Dynasty (c. 1650-1550 BCE) and ushering in the Second Intermediate Period. This tumultuous period would eventually give way to the rise of the New Kingdom, setting the stage for Egypt's imperial expansion and the zenith of its power and influence.

The Middle Kingdom was a period of reunification, prosperity, and cultural achievement, as Egypt emerged from the turmoil of the First Intermediate Period to forge a new era of unity and stability. The pharaohs of the Middle Kingdom expanded the nation's borders, developed trade and diplomatic relations, and fostered an environment in which art, literature, and architecture thrived.

The legacy of the Middle Kingdom endures in the form of its monumental architecture, literary masterpieces, and the enduring influence of its religious beliefs and practices. As we continue our exploration of Ancient Egypt's rich and diverse history, the Middle Kingdom serves as a testament to the resilience and adaptability of this remarkable civilization, and its ability to rise from the ashes of adversity to create a new era of prosperity and cultural achievement.

# CHAPTER 11: THE TWELFTH DYNASTY: EGYPT'S GOLDEN AGE

The Twelfth Dynasty (c. 1976-1793 BCE) represents the apex of the Middle Kingdom, an era characterised by political stability, economic prosperity, and cultural achievement. During this period, Egypt reached new heights in the realms of art, architecture, literature, and international relations, leaving a lasting legacy that would continue to shape the course of Egyptian history. In this chapter, we delve deeper into the various aspects of the Twelfth Dynasty, exploring the key events, figures, and accomplishments that defined Egypt's Golden Age.

The Founding of the Twelfth Dynasty: Amenemhat I

Amenemhat I (c. 1976-1947 BCE), the founder of the Twelfth Dynasty, came to power under somewhat uncertain circumstances, as he may have been a vizier during the Eleventh Dynasty. His rise to power marked a new era of centralised authority and strong kingship, which would set the tone for the rest of the dynasty. Amenemhat I established a new capital at Itjtawy, strategically located near the Faiyum Oasis, which facilitated the administration of the unified Egyptian state and promoted economic development.

Military Campaigns and Territorial Expansion

Under the Twelfth Dynasty, Egypt pursued an aggressive policy of territorial expansion and military conquest, particularly in Lower Nubia, the Levant, and Sinai. Pharaohs such as Senusret I (c. 1956-1911 BCE) and Senusret III (c. 1878-1860 BCE) led successful campaigns, subduing local tribes, securing valuable resources, and establishing a series of fortresses and trading posts to protect and maintain Egyptian interests.

The expansion of Egypt's borders during the Twelfth Dynasty facilitated the growth of international trade, as the nation established diplomatic and commercial ties with neighbouring regions. The wealth and prestige gained through these foreign relations further enhanced Egypt's status as a dominant regional power during its Golden Age.

Artistic and Cultural Achievements

The Twelfth Dynasty was marked by an efflorescence of artistic and cultural activity, as the patronage of the pharaohs and the relative peace and stability of the period fostered an environment conducive to creativity and innovation. Egyptian artists of this era experimented with new styles, techniques, and themes, resulting in a rich and diverse body of work that remains among the most celebrated in Egyptian history.

Sculpture, in particular, reached new heights during the Twelfth Dynasty, as craftsmen skillfully rendered their subjects in a more naturalistic and expressive manner. The colossal statues of Senusret III, which can be found at various sites across Egypt, are among the most iconic examples of Twelfth Dynasty sculpture, showcasing the technical mastery and artistic vision of their creators.

Literature also flourished during the Twelfth Dynasty, with the composition of numerous works that would become classics of Egyptian literature. Tales such as "The Tale of Sinuhe," "The Instruction of Amenemhat," and "The Story of the Shipwrecked Sailor" exemplify the literary achievements of this period, providing valuable insights into the concerns, values, and beliefs of Twelfth Dynasty society.

Architectural Wonders of the Twelfth Dynasty

The Twelfth Dynasty pharaohs were prolific builders, leaving behind an impressive array of architectural marvels that attest to their ambition and engineering prowess. While the pyramids of this period, such as those at Dahshur and Hawara, were less grandiose than their Old Kingdom predecessors, they nonetheless represent significant achievements in design and construction.

Temples, too, played a central role in Twelfth Dynasty architecture, with numerous complexes, such as the Temple of Karnak in Thebes, undergoing expansion and embellishment under the patronage of the dynasty's pharaohs. These temples not only served as centres of worship and religious instruction but also functioned as symbols of the state's power and authority, their grandiose design and intricate decoration reflecting the prestige and piety of their royal patrons.

In addition to religious structures, the Twelfth Dynasty also saw the construction of numerous palaces, administrative buildings, and fortresses, which served a variety of functions and helped to consolidate the pharaoh's control over the various regions of Egypt. These structures often featured innovative architectural elements, such as vaulted ceilings and decorative columns, which would have a lasting impact on the development of Egyptian architecture.

The End of the Twelfth Dynasty and the Legacy of Egypt's Golden Age

The Twelfth Dynasty came to an end around 1793 BCE, as a series of weak rulers, internal strife, and external pressures weakened the central government, paving the way for the Thirteenth Dynasty and the eventual onset of the Second Intermediate Period. Despite its relatively short duration, the Twelfth Dynasty left an indelible mark on Egyptian history, its achievements in the realms of art, architecture, literature, and diplomacy setting a high standard for subsequent generations to emulate.

The legacy of the Twelfth Dynasty can be seen in the continued prominence of the Middle Kingdom's artistic and architectural styles, which would have a lasting influence on the development of Egyptian visual culture. Furthermore, the expansion of Egypt's borders and the growth of international trade during this period laid the groundwork for the nation's rise to imperial power under the New Kingdom, a testament to the enduring impact of Egypt's Golden Age.

The Twelfth Dynasty represents a high point in the history of Ancient Egypt, an era of unparalleled artistic, cultural, and political achievement that would leave a lasting imprint on the sands of time. As we explore the various facets of this remarkable period, we gain a deeper appreciation for the ingenuity, creativity, and vision that defined Egypt's Golden Age, and the enduring legacy that continues to captivate and inspire us today.

to resonate with and inspire us today. The achievements of this period, from the captivating stories and moral teachings of its literature to the technical mastery and innovative spirit of its art, stand as a testament to the creativity, ingenuity, and wisdom of the Ancient Egyptians.

The growing emphasis on personal piety and the democratisation of the afterlife during the Middle Kingdom speaks to the evolving religious beliefs and aspirations of the Egyptian people, who sought not only to maintain order and balance in their earthly lives but also to secure a place in the eternal realm of the gods.

As we continue to study and appreciate the literature, art, and religion of the Middle Kingdom, we gain a deeper understanding of the complex and multifaceted culture that produced these enduring works, and the timeless values and ideals that shaped the lives of the men and women who inhabited this fascinating period in Egyptian history. By exploring the cultural achievements of the Middle Kingdom, we are afforded the opportunity to draw inspiration and wisdom from the past, enriching our own lives and deepening our connection to the eternal sands of Ancient Egypt.

# CHAPTER 12: THE HYKSOS INVASION: FOREIGN RULE IN EGYPT

The end of the Middle Kingdom marked the beginning of a tumultuous period in Egyptian history known as the Second Intermediate Period. This era, which lasted from approximately 1782 BCE to 1570 BCE, saw the fragmentation of Egypt into several competing kingdoms and the emergence of a foreign dynasty of rulers known as the Hyksos. In this chapter, we explore the rise and fall of the Hyksos, their impact on Egyptian society, and the legacy they left behind, as we continue our journey through the rich tapestry of Ancient Egyptian history.

The Rise of the Hyksos

The decline of the Middle Kingdom and the weakening of the central government created a power vacuum that would eventually be filled by a group of foreign invaders known as the Hyksos. Originating from Western Asia, the Hyksos entered Egypt during the Thirteenth Dynasty, taking advantage of the political instability and fragmentation that had gripped the country.

By the Fifteenth Dynasty, the Hyksos had established their capital at Avaris in the Nile Delta, from where they ruled over much of Lower Egypt. Their rule marked the first time in history that Egypt was governed by a foreign power, a development that would have far-reaching consequences for the nation's political, cultural, and military landscape.

Life Under Hyksos Rule

Despite their foreign origins, the Hyksos rulers adopted many aspects of Egyptian culture and administration, presenting themselves as legitimate pharaohs and incorporating Egyptian gods and religious practices into their own belief systems. This syncretism facilitated their rule over the local population, who continued to maintain their traditional way of life under the new regime.

Nevertheless, the Hyksos introduced several innovations to Egypt, most notably in the realms of technology and warfare. They were skilled horsemen and archers, and their introduction of the horse-drawn chariot, composite bow, and advanced bronze weaponry would have a lasting impact on Egyptian military strategy and tactics.

The Hyksos also brought with them new forms of art and craftsmanship, including pottery, jewellery, and textile production, which enriched and influenced Egyptian artistic traditions. Despite the challenges posed by foreign rule, this period of cultural exchange allowed for the transmission of ideas and techniques between the two civilizations, contributing to the evolution and development of Egyptian culture.

The Expulsion of the Hyksos and the Birth of the New Kingdom

The reign of the Hyksos was not without opposition, and their presence in Egypt galvanised the native population to resist foreign rule and seek reunification. The Seventeenth Dynasty, based in Thebes, led the struggle against the Hyksos, eventually culminating in the decisive military campaigns of Ahmose I, who successfully expelled the Hyksos from Egypt and reestablished a unified Egyptian state.

The defeat of the Hyksos marked the beginning of the Eighteenth Dynasty and the start of the New Kingdom, a period of unprecedented power and prosperity for Ancient Egypt. The experiences of the Second Intermediate Period and the Hyksos invasion had a profound impact on the nation's political and military outlook, with the pharaohs of the New Kingdom embarking on a series of ambitious military campaigns to secure their borders and expand their empire.

The Hyksos invasion and the Second Intermediate Period represent a critical juncture in the history of Ancient Egypt, a time of foreign rule, cultural exchange, and eventual national rebirth. Though the Hyksos were ultimately expelled from Egypt, their presence left an indelible mark on the nation's political, military, and cultural landscape, shaping the course of Egyptian history for centuries to come.

As we continue our exploration of Egypt's past, we are reminded of the resilience and adaptability of this remarkable civilization, which persevered through periods of turmoil and adversity to emerge stronger and more united than ever before. The story of the Hyksos invasion and the eventual reunification of Egypt under the New Kingdom serves as a testament to the enduring spirit and determination of the Egyptian people, who were able to rise above the challenges of their time and forge a new path towards greatness.

The legacy of the Hyksos invasion also highlights the complex interplay between foreign influence and indigenous culture, demonstrating how the exchange of ideas, technologies, and artistic traditions can enrich and transform a civilization, even during times of conflict and upheaval.

As we delve deeper into the history of the New Kingdom in the coming chapters, we will see how the lessons learned and the innovations introduced during the Second Intermediate Period and the Hyksos rule laid the groundwork for an era of unprecedented expansion, wealth, and artistic achievement, firmly establishing Ancient Egypt as one of the most powerful and influential empires of the ancient world.

# CHAPTER 13: THE NEW KINGDOM: THE EGYPTIAN EMPIRE

The New Kingdom, which spanned from around 1570 BCE to 1070 BCE, marked a new era of power, wealth, and cultural achievement for Ancient Egypt. Following the expulsion of the Hyksos and the reunification of the country under the Eighteenth Dynasty, Egypt embarked on an ambitious program of territorial expansion and imperial consolidation, transforming itself into one of the most formidable empires of the ancient world. In this chapter, we will explore the rise and fall of the Egyptian Empire, the remarkable achievements of its pharaohs, and the enduring legacy of this golden age of Egyptian history.

The Expansion of the Egyptian Empire

The pharaohs of the New Kingdom were determined to prevent a repeat of the foreign invasions that had plagued Egypt during the Second Intermediate Period. As such, they pursued an aggressive policy of territorial expansion, extending their influence far beyond the traditional boundaries of Egypt and securing vital resources and strategic footholds in neighbouring regions.

Under the reigns of Thutmose I, Thutmose III, and Amenhotep II, Egypt expanded its empire to encompass vast territories in Nubia, the Levant, and the eastern Mediterranean. These conquests brought immense wealth and power to the Egyptian state, as well as a steady flow of tribute, slaves, and resources from the subjugated regions. The imperial ambitions of the New Kingdom pharaohs transformed Egypt into a true superpower, one whose influence and prestige were felt across the ancient world.

The zenith of Egyptian imperial power came during the reign of Ramesses II, who is often considered the most powerful and successful pharaoh of the New Kingdom. Ramesses II's military campaigns and diplomatic efforts cemented Egypt's dominance in the region, culminating in the famous Battle of Kadesh against the Hittites and the subsequent signing of the world's first recorded peace treaty.

Art and Culture during the New Kingdom

The New Kingdom was a period of unparalleled cultural and artistic achievement for Ancient Egypt. The wealth and resources that flowed into the country as a result of its imperial conquests fueled a renaissance of creativity and innovation, as artists, architects, and craftsmen pushed the boundaries of their crafts in service of the pharaohs and the gods.

The grand temples and monuments of the New Kingdom, such as the Temple of Karnak, the Temple of Luxor, and the mortuary temples of Hatshepsut and Ramesses II, are among the most impressive and enduring examples of ancient Egyptian architecture. These monumental structures served as testaments to the power and piety of the pharaohs, as well as vital centres of religious, political, and economic activity.

The art of the New Kingdom was marked by a renewed emphasis on realism and naturalism, with artists striving to capture the subtleties of human expression and the intricacies of the natural world in their works. This can be seen in the exquisite wall paintings, relief sculptures, and statues that adorned the temples and tombs of the era, their lifelike forms and vibrant colours capturing the essence of the world around them.

The Decline of the Egyptian Empire

Despite the immense power and prosperity of the New Kingdom, the empire eventually succumbed to the forces of decline and disintegration. The later pharaohs of the Twentieth Dynasty faced numerous internal and external challenges, including economic stagnation, social unrest, and the rise of powerful rival states in the Near East.

The fall of the New Kingdom marked the end of Egypt's imperial ambitions, as the country entered a period of political fragmentation and foreign domination known as the Third Intermediate Period. However, the legacy of the Egyptian Empire would continue to resonate throughout the ancient world, its achievements and influence serving as a source of inspiration and admiration for generations to come.

Legacy of the New Kingdom

The impact of the New Kingdom on the course of Egyptian history and the wider ancient world cannot be overstated. It was a period of immense political, economic, and cultural achievement that left an indelible mark on the sands of time. The legacy of the New Kingdom can be seen in various aspects of ancient Egyptian society and beyond.

The accomplishments of the New Kingdom pharaohs, particularly their military prowess and diplomatic acumen, set a new standard for rulership in the ancient world. The tales of their exploits, such as Thutmose III's campaigns or Ramesses II's victory at the Battle of Kadesh, would be recounted and studied for generations, inspiring leaders and strategists alike.

The artistic and architectural innovations of the New Kingdom had a lasting impact on Egyptian culture, shaping the development of art and architecture for centuries to come. The realism and naturalism that characterised New Kingdom art would become hallmarks of Egyptian artistic expression, while the monumental scale and grandeur of its architecture would continue to inspire awe and admiration.

The religious developments of the New Kingdom, such as

the cult of Amun and the short-lived Amarna Period under Akhenaten, also had a profound influence on Egyptian religious thought and practice. These shifts in religious beliefs and practices would shape the spiritual landscape of Ancient Egypt, leaving an indelible mark on its people and their relationship with the divine.

The New Kingdom's decline serves as a cautionary tale of the fragility of power and the cyclical nature of history. Despite its immense wealth and influence, the Egyptian Empire was ultimately unable to withstand the forces of change that would bring about its downfall. This lesson in the ephemerality of power would be a recurring theme throughout the history of human civilization, a reminder of the need for humility, adaptability, and foresight in the face of an ever-changing world.

The New Kingdom was a period of triumph and tragedy, a time when Ancient Egypt reached its pinnacle of power, wealth, and cultural achievement, only to succumb to the inexorable forces of decline and disintegration. The story of the Egyptian Empire serves as a window into the complex tapestry of human history, revealing the heights of greatness that can be achieved, as well as the challenges and pitfalls that even the most powerful empires must face.

As we continue our journey through the annals of Ancient Egypt, we will explore the subsequent periods of fragmentation, resurgence, and foreign domination that would come to define the nation's later history. Through it all, the enduring legacy of the New Kingdom, with its tales of conquest, innovation, and artistic brilliance, will serve as a constant reminder of the indomitable spirit and creative genius of the Egyptian people.

# CHAPTER 14: THE EIGHTEENTH DYNASTY: EGYPT'S AGE OF EMPIRE

The Eighteenth Dynasty, spanning from around 1550 BCE to 1292 BCE, marked the beginning of the New Kingdom and the rise of Egypt as a global superpower. This period witnessed a series of powerful and charismatic pharaohs who expanded the empire's borders, built magnificent monuments, and left an indelible mark on Egyptian history. In this chapter, we will explore the key events, rulers, and achievements of the Eighteenth Dynasty, highlighting the factors that contributed to Egypt's ascent to imperial greatness.

The Rise of the Eighteenth Dynasty

The Eighteenth Dynasty began with the reunification of Egypt under the leadership of Ahmose I, who expelled the Hyksos rulers from the Nile Delta and restored native Egyptian rule. The subsequent pharaohs of the Eighteenth Dynasty built on this foundation, consolidating their power and embarking on ambitious military campaigns to extend Egypt's sphere of influence.

Pharaohs such as Thutmose I and Thutmose III led Egypt in conquering vast territories in Nubia, the Levant, and the eastern Mediterranean. These conquests brought immense wealth, resources, and prestige to the Egyptian state, fueling a period of cultural and artistic renaissance.

Notable Pharaohs of the Eighteenth Dynasty

Ahmose I (c. 1550 - 1525 BCE): As mentioned earlier, Ahmose I was the founder of the Eighteenth Dynasty, and he played a pivotal role in reunifying Egypt after the expulsion of the

Hyksos. His reign marked the beginning of the New Kingdom era and laid the groundwork for Egypt's rise as an imperial power.

Hatshepsut (c. 1479 - 1458 BCE): One of the few female pharaohs in Egyptian history, Hatshepsut reigned for over two decades and was known for her ambitious building projects, including her mortuary temple at Deir el-Bahri. Her reign was marked by peace and prosperity, and she focused on expanding trade and diplomacy rather than military conquest.

Thutmose III (c. 1479 - 1425 BCE): Known as the "Napoleon of Egypt," Thutmose III was a skilled military strategist who led Egypt to numerous victories, expanding its empire to its greatest territorial extent. His reign was also marked by extensive building projects, particularly at the Temple of Karnak.

Amenhotep III (c. 1388 - 1351 BCE): Amenhotep III's reign was a period of unprecedented wealth and artistic achievement for Egypt. He was a great patron of the arts and initiated numerous building projects, including the Colossi of Memnon and the Luxor Temple. His reign marked the height of Egypt's power and prestige in the ancient world.

Akhenaten (c. 1353 - 1336 BCE): The enigmatic pharaoh Akhenaten is perhaps best known for his religious revolution, during which he attempted to replace the traditional Egyptian pantheon with the worship of the sun disk, Aten. His reign, known as the Amarna Period, saw a radical transformation in Egyptian art and culture, as well as the construction of a new capital city at Amarna.

Tutankhamun (c. 1332 - 1323 BCE): The young pharaoh Tutankhamun is famous for his well-preserved tomb, discovered by Howard Carter in 1922. His reign marked a return to traditional Egyptian religious practices following the upheaval of the Amarna Period.

Cultural and Artistic Achievements

The Eighteenth Dynasty was marked by a flourishing of art, architecture, and culture, as the wealth and resources gained from Egypt's imperial expansion fueled a period of creative innovation and experimentation. The increased contact with foreign cultures, particularly those of the Levant, the Aegean, and the Near East, brought new artistic styles, techniques, and motifs into Egyptian art.

One of the most striking features of Eighteenth Dynasty art was its increased naturalism and attention to detail, as artists sought to portray their subjects with greater realism and individuality. This can be seen in the famous bust of Nefertiti, the wife of Akhenaten, which showcases the sculptor's skill in capturing the subtle nuances of the queen's facial features and expression.

Another significant development of this period was the proliferation of large-scale building projects, as pharaohs sought to immortalise their reigns through the construction of monumental temples, tombs, and palaces. Notable examples include Hatshepsut's mortuary temple at Deir el-Bahri, the vast temple complex at Karnak, and the Luxor Temple built by Amenhotep III.

The religious innovations of the Amarna Period also had a profound impact on Egyptian art and culture, as artists were encouraged to break with traditional conventions and explore new forms of artistic expression. The distinctive Amarna style, characterised by elongated, curvilinear forms and a focus on the intimate, personal aspects of the divine, represented a radical departure from the formalism and idealisation of earlier Egyptian art.

The End of the Eighteenth Dynasty and the Legacy of the Age of Empire

The Eighteenth Dynasty came to an end with the reign of Horemheb, a military general who became pharaoh and sought to restore the traditional order following the upheaval of the Amarna Period. His efforts to erase the memory of Akhenaten and his successors, known as the "Amarna backlash," marked a return to the conservative religious and artistic practices of the pre-Amarna era.

Despite the turbulence and change that characterised the Eighteenth Dynasty, its legacy as Egypt's Age of Empire remains a defining chapter in the nation's history. The achievements of its rulers, from the military conquests of Thutmose III to the artistic innovations of the Amarna Period, left a lasting impact on Egyptian art, culture, and society. The monumental temples, tombs, and palaces that were constructed during this era continue to inspire awe and admiration, bearing witness to the indomitable spirit and creative genius of the ancient Egyptians.

As we move forward in our journey through the annals of Ancient Egypt, we will explore the subsequent dynasties of the New Kingdom, delving into the lives and accomplishments of the pharaohs who continued to shape the course of Egyptian history. Through it all, the enduring legacy of the Eighteenth Dynasty serves as a reminder of the heights of greatness that can be achieved when a civilization harnesses its collective strength, ambition, and creativity.

# CHAPTER 15: AKHENATEN AND THE AMARNA PERIOD: A TIME OF RELIGIOUS UPHEAVAL

The Amarna Period, which took place during the reign of the enigmatic Pharaoh Akhenaten, is perhaps one of the most intriguing and debated chapters in ancient Egyptian history. This relatively short period, lasting from around 1353 to 1336 BCE, witnessed a radical transformation in Egyptian religion, art, and culture, as Akhenaten sought to replace the traditional pantheon of gods with the worship of a single deity, the Aten. In this chapter, we will delve into the life and reign of Akhenaten, the revolutionary changes he instituted, and the lasting impact of the Amarna Period on Egyptian history.

The Life and Reign of Akhenaten

Born as Amenhotep IV, the son of Amenhotep III and Queen Tiye, Akhenaten ascended the throne at a time of unprecedented wealth and power for Egypt. Early in his reign, he began to introduce a series of religious reforms, which culminated in the establishment of the Aten, the sun disk, as the supreme and sole deity of Egypt.

In order to consolidate his religious revolution, Akhenaten moved the capital from Thebes to a newly constructed city called Akhetaten (modern-day Amarna), which was dedicated to the worship of the Aten. The move was a strategic decision, as Thebes was the centre of the powerful Amun priesthood, which posed a threat to Akhenaten's new religious order.

The Religious Revolution

The worship of the Aten marked a dramatic departure from the traditional polytheistic religion of Egypt, which recognized a vast pantheon of gods and goddesses. The Aten was portrayed as an all-encompassing, omnipotent deity that transcended the physical realm, with Akhenaten and his queen, Nefertiti, serving as the sole intermediaries between the Aten and the Egyptian people.

This new monotheistic religion sought to undermine the traditional cults and priesthoods that had dominated Egyptian society for centuries, as the temples and rituals dedicated to the old gods were gradually abandoned or repurposed in favor of the Aten. The extent to which this religious revolution was embraced by the wider population remains a subject of debate among historians, with some suggesting that it was largely confined to the royal court and the elite.

The Art of the Amarna Period

One of the most striking aspects of the Amarna Period was its distinctive artistic style, which broke with the conventions and formalism of traditional Egyptian art. The Amarna style was characterized by a greater degree of naturalism, as artists sought to portray their subjects, including the royal family, with more individuality and realism.

The art of this period also reflected the central tenets of the new religion, with an emphasis on the intimate, personal aspects of the divine. Scenes depicting Akhenaten and Nefertiti worshipping the Aten, or engaged in familial activities with their children, became common motifs, showcasing the radical shift in artistic themes and values.

The End of the Amarna Period and the Restoration of the Old Religion

The Amarna Period came to an abrupt end following the death of Akhenaten, and Egypt witnessed a period of restoration under his successors, Tutankhamun and Horemheb. The old religion was reinstated, and the worship of the Aten was abandoned, as the traditional gods and goddesses were once again embraced by the Egyptian people.

The city of Amarna was gradually abandoned, and the temples, monuments, and inscriptions associated with the Aten and the royal family were systematically dismantled or defaced. This "Amarna backlash" was an attempt to erase the memory of Akhenaten's religious revolution and restore the traditional order that had defined Egyptian society for centuries.

The Legacy of the Amarna Period

Despite the efforts to erase the memory of Akhenaten and his religious reforms, the Amarna Period has continued to captivate the imagination of historians, archaeologists, and the general public alike. The radical changes that took place during this time, both in terms of religion and art, have provided a unique window into the complexities and challenges faced by ancient Egyptian society.

The Amarna Period has also fueled numerous debates and speculations regarding the motivations, beliefs, and ultimate fate of Akhenaten and his family. Some historians have hailed him as a visionary who sought to promote a more egalitarian, monotheistic faith, while others view him as a heretic who disrupted the social and religious order for his own self-aggrandizement.

The art of the Amarna Period, despite its relatively short duration, has had a lasting impact on the history of Egyptian art. The increased naturalism and attention to detail that characterized this era would continue to influence Egyptian artists for generations to come, as they sought to balance the traditional ideals of harmony and order with the desire for individual expression and realism.

The Amarna Period remains one of the most enigmatic and fascinating chapters in ancient Egyptian history, its revolutionary ideas and artistic innovations standing in stark contrast to the millennia of tradition that preceded and followed it. As we continue our journey through the annals of ancient Egypt, we are reminded of the power of individuals and ideas to shape the course of history, and the enduring allure of the mysteries and intrigues that lie buried beneath the sands of time.

# CHAPTER 16: THE NINETEENTH DYNASTY: THE RAMESSIDE ERA

The Nineteenth Dynasty, also known as the Ramesside Era, was a period of renewed power and prosperity for ancient Egypt. Lasting from around 1292 to 1189 BCE, this dynasty was marked by the reigns of several powerful pharaohs, including Ramses I, Seti I, and the legendary Ramses II. In this chapter, we will explore the major events, achievements, and challenges that defined this remarkable period in Egyptian history.

The Founding of the Nineteenth Dynasty: Ramses I and Seti I

The Nineteenth Dynasty was founded by Ramses I, a military commander who was appointed as the vizier and later the heir to the throne by the last pharaoh of the Eighteenth Dynasty, Horemheb. Ramses I ruled for a brief two-year period, but his reign marked the beginning of a new era of stability and expansion for Egypt.

Seti I, the son of Ramses I, succeeded his father and embarked on a series of ambitious military campaigns to reassert Egyptian control over lost territories in the Levant and Nubia. Seti I also focused on the internal affairs of Egypt, launching a number of building projects, including the completion of the Hypostyle Hall in the Karnak Temple, and the construction of his own mortuary temple and tomb in the Valley of the Kings.

The Reign of Ramses II: The Great Builder

Ramses II, also known as Ramses the Great, was the third pharaoh of the Nineteenth Dynasty and one of the most powerful and celebrated rulers in ancient Egyptian history. His reign, which lasted for 66 years, saw Egypt reach new heights of wealth, power, and architectural achievement.

One of the most significant aspects of Ramses II's reign was his extensive building program, which included the construction of numerous temples, monuments, and cities throughout Egypt and its conquered territories. Among his most famous projects were the Great Temple of Abu Simbel, the Ramesseum at Thebes, and the city of Pi-Ramesses, which served as the new capital of Egypt during his reign.

Military Campaigns and Diplomacy

Ramses II is also known for his military campaigns, most notably his battles against the Hittites, a powerful kingdom in Anatolia (modern-day Turkey). The Battle of Kadesh, fought in 1274 BCE, was a pivotal moment in the conflict between Egypt and the Hittites. Although the battle ended in a stalemate, Ramses II claimed it as a great victory and had the events of the battle inscribed on the walls of his temples, including the temples at Abu Simbel and Karnak.

After years of conflict, Ramses II and the Hittite king, Hattusili III, negotiated a historic peace treaty, which is considered to be the world's first recorded peace treaty. This agreement not only brought an end to hostilities between the two powers but also established a lasting alliance that allowed both kingdoms to prosper and focus on internal affairs.

Family Life and Succession

Ramses II was known to have had several wives, including his Great Royal Wife, Nefertari, as well as numerous children. The royal family played a prominent role in the religious and political life of Egypt, with many of Ramses II's sons and daughters holding important positions within the government and the priesthood.

When Ramses II finally passed away at the age of 90, his thirteenth son, Merenptah, succeeded him to the throne. The later pharaohs of the Nineteenth Dynasty faced numerous challenges, including internal strife and external threats, but the legacy of the Ramess side Era would continue to shape the course of Egyptian history for generations to come.

The Later Pharaohs of the Nineteenth Dynasty

Following the death of Ramses II, the Nineteenth Dynasty entered a period of decline, characterized by a series of short-lived reigns and increasing instability. Merenptah, the successor of Ramses II, faced invasions from the Libyans and the mysterious Sea Peoples, which he managed to repel, preserving Egypt's borders and maintaining a semblance of stability.

However, subsequent pharaohs, such as Seti II, Siptah, and Tausret, struggled to maintain control over the kingdom, as the once-powerful Egyptian state began to fracture under the weight of internal conflicts and external pressures.

The Fall of the Nineteenth Dynasty and the Rise of the Twentieth Dynasty

The final pharaoh of the Nineteenth Dynasty, a usurper named Setnakhte, seized power amidst the chaos and sought to restore order to the kingdom. His short reign was marked by efforts to reestablish the authority of the central government and to complete unfinished building projects, but he was unable to fully reverse the decline that had taken hold of Egypt.

Setnakhte's son, Ramses III, would go on to found the Twentieth Dynasty, marking the end of the Ramesside Era and the beginning of a new chapter in ancient Egyptian history.

The Nineteenth Dynasty, and the Ramesside Era as a whole, was a period of great achievement and ambition for ancient Egypt. From the military conquests of Seti I and Ramses II to the monumental building projects that transformed the landscape of Egypt, this era saw the kingdom reach new heights of power and glory.

However, the decline that followed the death of Ramses II serves as a poignant reminder of the fragility of even the most powerful and enduring empires. As we continue our exploration of ancient Egyptian history, we are reminded of the complex interplay of forces that shaped this remarkable civilization, and the lasting impact of the individuals and events that defined its rise and fall.

# CHAPTER 17: THE TWENTIETH DYNASTY: THE DECLINE OF THE NEW KINGDOM

The Twentieth Dynasty, the final dynasty of the New Kingdom, marked a period of decline and fragmentation for ancient Egypt. Although it began with the reign of the capable Ramses III, it would ultimately be characterized by a series of weak pharaohs, internal strife, and external pressures that hastened the end of the New Kingdom. In this chapter, we will examine the key events and factors that contributed to the decline of this once-great civilization.

The Reign of Ramses III: The Last Great Pharaoh

Ramses III, the founder of the Twentieth Dynasty, is often considered the last great pharaoh of the New Kingdom. His reign, which lasted from 1189 to 1155 BCE, was marked by significant military victories against Egypt's enemies, most notably the Sea Peoples and the Libyans. However, despite his successes on the battlefield, Ramses III faced increasing challenges in maintaining control over the sprawling Egyptian state.

In addition to external threats, Ramses III's reign was also marked by economic difficulties, as the cost of maintaining Egypt's extensive military, administrative, and religious infrastructure strained the kingdom's resources. To compound these issues, a series of droughts and crop failures led to widespread food shortages and social unrest, further eroding the stability of the kingdom.

The Harem Conspiracy and the Succession Crisis

Towards the end of Ramses III's reign, a major conspiracy known as the Harem Conspiracy was uncovered within the royal court. The plot, which was led by one of Ramses III's secondary wives, Queen Tiye, aimed to assassinate the pharaoh and place her son, Pentawer, on the throne. While the conspiracy ultimately failed, and the perpetrators were punished, the incident revealed the growing instability and intrigue that characterized the later years of the New Kingdom.

Following Ramses III's death, a succession crisis ensued, as his designated heir, Ramses IV, faced challenges from rival claimants to the throne. This crisis marked the beginning of a pattern of short and troubled reigns that would come to define the Twentieth Dynasty.

A Series of Weak Pharaohs and the Erosion of Royal Power

The later pharaohs of the Twentieth Dynasty, including Ramses IV, Ramses V, and Ramses VI, struggled to maintain control over the kingdom as the power of the central government waned. In the face of economic challenges and growing unrest, these pharaohs were unable to undertake the ambitious building projects that had characterized earlier periods of Egyptian history, and the influence of the pharaohs diminished in comparison to that of powerful local officials and priests.

The rise of the Amun priesthood in Thebes, in particular, contributed to the erosion of royal power, as the priests gained increasing control over the temples and their vast resources. This shift in power would have significant implications for the future of Egypt, as the central government became less able to respond effectively to internal and external challenges.

The Collapse of the New Kingdom

As the Twentieth Dynasty drew to a close, the various factors that had contributed to the decline of the New Kingdom coalesced into a perfect storm of crisis and collapse. The kingdom was beset by a series of invasions, including those by the Libyans, the Nubians, and the Assyrians, which further weakened the already fragile state.

The final pharaoh of the Twentieth Dynasty, Ramses XI, faced numerous challenges, including a major civil war known as the Suppression of the High Priest of Amun. This conflict, which pitted the forces of the pharaoh against the powerful priesthood, further weakened the already fractured kingdom.

Ultimately, the New Kingdom would come to an end with the death of Ramses XI and the dissolution of the central government. Egypt would enter a new period of fragmentation and decline, known as the Third Intermediate Period, in which regional powers, foreign invaders, and ambitious priests would vie for control over the once-great kingdom.

The Twentieth Dynasty and the decline of the New Kingdom serve as a poignant reminder of the cyclical nature of history and the challenges faced by even the most powerful and enduring empires. The convergence of internal strife, external pressures, and economic difficulties ultimately led to the collapse of the New Kingdom, marking the end of a golden age of Egyptian history.

As we continue our exploration of ancient Egypt, we are reminded of the complex interplay of factors that shaped the rise and fall of this remarkable civilization, and the lasting impact of the individuals and events that defined its history. The decline of the New Kingdom provides valuable insights into the fragility of human societies and the forces that can drive even the most successful states to the brink of collapse.

# CHAPTER 18: THE THIRD INTERMEDIATE PERIOD: A TIME OF FRAGMENTATION

The Third Intermediate Period, spanning from the end of the Twentieth Dynasty in 1070 BCE to the beginning of the Late Period in 664 BCE, was a time of political fragmentation, social upheaval, and cultural transformation in ancient Egypt. The centralized power of the pharaohs had weakened significantly, giving rise to a number of competing local rulers and foreign powers who vied for control over the Nile Valley. In this chapter, we will delve into the key events, figures, and dynamics that defined this tumultuous era in Egyptian history.

The Emergence of Regional Powers

With the collapse of the New Kingdom and the central government, Egypt became divided among various regional powers. The north was controlled by the kings of Tanis, who formed the Twenty-first Dynasty, while the south was under the sway of the High Priests of Amun in Thebes, who established the Twenty-second Dynasty. These rival factions would engage in a series of power struggles and conflicts that would further fragment the once-unified kingdom.

During the Twenty-second Dynasty, the pharaohs of Libyan descent ruled from the city of Bubastis. Although they managed to maintain a semblance of unity and authority, their rule was often challenged by powerful regional governors and other factions, leading to ongoing instability throughout the land.

The Kushite Conquest and the Twenty-fifth Dynasty

In the Eighth Century BCE, the Kingdom of Kush, located in modern-day Sudan, emerged as a powerful regional player. The Kushite kings, who had long admired Egyptian culture and traditions, sought to restore the unity and greatness of Egypt by launching a series of military campaigns into the Nile Valley.

Under the leadership of King Piye, the Kushites successfully conquered Egypt and established the Twenty-fifth Dynasty. Piye and his successors, including Taharqa and Tantamani, sought to revitalize Egyptian culture and religion, as well as embarking on ambitious building projects that harkened back to the grandeur of the New Kingdom. However, their reign would be short-lived, as the growing power of the Assyrian Empire threatened to engulf the region.

The Assyrian Invasion and the Twenty-sixth Dynasty

The Assyrians, under the leadership of kings such as Esarhaddon and Ashurbanipal, launched a series of invasions into Egypt during the late Twenty-fifth Dynasty, ultimately defeating the Kushites and installing their own puppet rulers in the Nile Valley. This period of Assyrian domination was deeply resented by the Egyptians and would have a lasting impact on the region's political dynamics.

Eventually, the native Egyptian ruler Psamtik I, with the help of Greek mercenaries, managed to expel the Assyrians from Egypt and establish the Twenty-sixth Dynasty, also known as the Saite Dynasty, in reference to their capital city of Sais. This marked the beginning of the Late Period, which will be explored in greater detail in the following chapters.

The Third Intermediate Period was a time of fragmentation and upheaval for ancient Egypt, as the once-mighty civilization struggled to maintain its unity and identity in the face of internal divisions and external threats. Despite these challenges, the period also witnessed the resilience and adaptability of the Egyptian people, as well as the enduring allure of their cultural and religious traditions.

As we continue our journey through the history of ancient Egypt, we will explore the ways in which the events and dynamics of the Third Intermediate Period would shape the trajectory of the Late Period and the final chapters of Egypt's ancient history.

# CHAPTER 19: THE LATE PERIOD: EGYPT'S FINAL RESURGENCE

The Late Period, spanning from 664 BCE to 332 BCE, marked the final chapter of ancient Egypt's native rule before the arrival of Alexander the Great and the subsequent Ptolemaic Dynasty. The period witnessed a resurgence of Egyptian power and culture, as well as the ongoing struggle to maintain independence in the face of growing foreign influence. In this chapter, we will explore the key events, figures, and developments that characterized the Late Period, shedding light on the final centuries of ancient Egypt's native rule.

The Twenty-sixth Dynasty: The Saite Renaissance

The Twenty-sixth Dynasty, also known as the Saite Dynasty, marked a period of renewed vigor and prosperity for Egypt, as the kings of Sais sought to restore the country's unity, prestige, and cultural vitality. Under the leadership of Pharaohs such as Psamtik I, Necho II, and Apries, the Saite kings undertook ambitious building projects, military campaigns, and diplomatic initiatives to strengthen their power and assert their authority over the Nile Valley.

The Saite Renaissance saw a revival of traditional Egyptian art, architecture, and religious practices, as the ruling elite looked back to the glories of the past for inspiration and guidance. This period also witnessed the increasing influence of Greek culture and trade, as the Egyptians sought to build alliances and expand their horizons in the face of a rapidly changing world.

The Persian Conquest and the Twenty-seventh Dynasty

The rise of the Achaemenid Persian Empire, under the

leadership of Cyrus the Great and his successors, would ultimately bring an end to the Saite Dynasty and usher in a new era of foreign rule in Egypt. In 525 BCE, the Persian king Cambyses II launched a successful invasion of Egypt, defeating the Saite ruler Psamtik III and incorporating the Nile Valley into the vast Persian Empire.

The Persian conquest marked the beginning of the Twenty-seventh Dynasty, during which Egypt was governed by Persian satraps and experienced varying degrees of political autonomy and cultural integration. While the Egyptians were allowed to maintain their religious practices and institutions, the Persian rulers sought to exert their authority and control over the region through a combination of military force, taxation, and administrative reforms.

The Late Period: Egypt's Struggle for Independence

Throughout the Late Period, Egypt would experience periods of independence and foreign domination, as native rulers and foreign powers vied for control over the Nile Valley. The Twenty-eighth, Twenty-ninth, and Thirtieth Dynasties represented brief interludes of native Egyptian rule, during which the kings of Mendes, Sebennytos, and Hermopolis sought to restore Egypt's independence and resist the encroachment of foreign powers.

However, these efforts would ultimately prove unsuccessful, as the Persian Empire reasserted its control over Egypt during the Thirty-first Dynasty, leading to the final Persian domination of Egypt. This period of foreign rule would come to an end with the arrival of Alexander the Great in 332 BCE, marking the beginning of the Greco-Roman Period and a new chapter in Egypt's storied history.

The Late Period of ancient Egypt was a time of struggle, resilience, and transformation, as the native rulers and foreign powers battled for control over the Nile Valley and the cultural, religious, and political identity of the Egyptian people. This period, often overshadowed by the earlier glories of the Old, Middle, and New Kingdoms, provides valuable insights into the enduring legacy of ancient Egypt and the forces that shaped its final chapters.

As we move forward in our exploration of ancient Egypt's history, we will examine the Greco-Roman Period and the ways in which the arrival of Alexander the Great and the subsequent Ptolemaic Dynasty would further shape the development of Egyptian culture, society, and politics. We will delve into the complex interactions between the native Egyptian population and the Greek and Roman settlers who would come to dominate the region for centuries, and how these exchanges influenced the course of history.

The Late Period, although marked by political turmoil and foreign domination, also witnessed moments of cultural renaissance and political resurgence, as native Egyptian rulers sought to revive and maintain their rich cultural heritage in the face of overwhelming odds. The determination and resilience of the Egyptian people during this time serves as a testament to the enduring strength of their civilization, which would continue to adapt and evolve even as it entered a new era of Greco-Roman influence.

Ultimately, the Late Period provides a fascinating window into the dynamic and ever-changing landscape of ancient Egypt, and serves as a crucial link between the world of the pharaohs and the world of the Ptolemies and Roman emperors. Through an understanding of this often-overlooked period, we can gain a more complete and nuanced appreciation for the extraordinary story of ancient Egypt and its enduring impact on the course of human history.

# CHAPTER 20: THE TWENTY-SIXTH DYNASTY: THE SAITE RENAISSANCE

The Twenty-sixth Dynasty, also known as the Saite Dynasty, represents a remarkable period in ancient Egypt's history, characterized by cultural revival, political resurgence, and economic prosperity. Spanning from 664 BCE to 525 BCE, this dynasty saw native Egyptian rulers emerge from the shadows of foreign domination and work tirelessly to reestablish the country's unity, prestige, and cultural vitality. In this chapter, we will delve into the fascinating history of the Saite Renaissance, exploring the key events, figures, and achievements that defined this dynamic era.

The Rise of the Saite Dynasty

The origins of the Twenty-sixth Dynasty can be traced back to the waning years of the Third Intermediate Period, when Egypt was fragmented and under the control of various local rulers and foreign powers. In the city of Sais, located in the western Delta, a powerful family emerged as a force to be reckoned with. Psamtik I, the founder of the Saite Dynasty, rose to power in 664 BCE after the Assyrians withdrew from Egypt, leaving a power vacuum in their wake.

With the support of Greek mercenaries, Psamtik I managed to consolidate his rule over the entire Nile Valley, bringing an end to decades of political fragmentation and chaos. Under Psamtik's leadership, Egypt once again became a centralized state with a strong, unified government.

Cultural Revival and the Influence of Greek Culture

One of the most notable aspects of the Saite Renaissance was the reinvigoration of traditional Egyptian art, architecture, and religious practices. Saite pharaohs sought to emulate the grandeur and cultural achievements of the Old, Middle, and New Kingdoms, and they heavily invested in monumental building projects, including the construction of new temples, tombs, and palaces.

Artists and craftsmen during the Saite period adopted and refined the artistic conventions and techniques of earlier periods, with a particular focus on intricate relief work and detailed statuary. The Saite Dynasty's dedication to cultural revival extended to the realm of religious life, as the worship of ancient Egyptian gods such as Osiris, Amun, and Hathor experienced a resurgence.

At the same time, the Saite Dynasty was also marked by significant Greek influence, particularly in the realm of trade and diplomacy. Greek merchants and mercenaries played an essential role in the revitalization of Egypt's economy and the consolidation of its military power. The city of Naukratis, founded by the Greeks in the 7th century BCE, became a major hub of trade and cultural exchange between Egypt and the Greek world.

Key Figures and Achievements

Several notable pharaohs defined the Saite Dynasty, leaving lasting legacies that would shape the course of Egyptian history. Psamtik I, the founder of the dynasty, was instrumental in unifying Egypt and initiating the Saite Renaissance. His ambitious building projects, military campaigns, and diplomatic initiatives set the stage for the achievements of his successors.

Necho II, the son of Psamtik I, was a visionary ruler who sought to expand Egypt's influence in the Mediterranean world. He is perhaps best known for his ambitious, albeit unsuccessful, attempt to dig a canal connecting the Nile to the

Red Sea, a precursor to the modern Suez Canal. Necho II also launched a series of military campaigns in the Levant, briefly reestablishing Egyptian control over territories lost during the Third Intermediate Period.

Apries, another significant Saite pharaoh, is remembered for his extensive building projects, including the reconstruction and expansion of the Temple of Amun at Karnak. Apries also led military campaigns in the Levant and Libya, though his reign ultimately ended in turmoil due to a disastrous campaign against the Greek city of Cy rene and a subsequent rebellion led by his own general, Amasis II.

Amasis II, who ascended to the throne after overthrowing Apries, proved to be a capable and popular ruler. He focused on strengthening Egypt's economy by encouraging trade with the Greek world and fostering the growth of Naukratis as a major trading hub. Amasis II also embarked on an ambitious building program, which included the construction of the Temple of Horus at Edfu and the Temple of Neith in Sais. His reign was marked by relative peace and prosperity, as he successfully navigated the complex geopolitical landscape of the Mediterranean world.

The End of the Saite Dynasty and the Persian Conquest

Despite the achievements and resilience of the Saite pharaohs, the Twenty-sixth Dynasty ultimately succumbed to the rising power of the Achaemenid Persian Empire. In 525 BCE, the Persian king Cambyses II launched an invasion of Egypt, taking advantage of internal strife and a weakened military following the reign of the last Saite pharaoh, Psamtik III.

The Persians defeated Psamtik III at the Battle of Pelusium and swiftly conquered Egypt, incorporating the Nile Valley into their vast empire. The fall of the Saite Dynasty marked the end of the native Egyptian rule and the beginning of a tumultuous period in Egyptian history characterized by foreign domination and struggle for independence.

The Twenty-sixth Dynasty, or the Saite Renaissance, stands as a testament to the enduring strength and resilience of ancient Egyptian civilization. During this dynamic period, native Egyptian rulers managed to restore unity, prosperity, and cultural vitality to a fragmented and weakened nation. The Saite pharaohs' dedication to the preservation and revitalization of their ancestral culture, coupled with their openness to foreign influence and trade, allowed Egypt to adapt and thrive in a rapidly changing world.

Although the Saite Dynasty ultimately succumbed to the powerful Persian Empire, its legacy would continue to shape the course of Egyptian history, leaving a lasting impression on the cultural, political, and economic landscape of the ancient world. The achievements and struggles of the Saite pharaohs serve as a valuable reminder of the complexities and triumphs of human civilization, offering rich insights into the indomitable spirit of ancient Egypt.

# CHAPTER 21: THE PERSIAN CONQUEST AND THE TWENTY-SEVENTH DYNASTY

The Persian conquest of Egypt in 525 BCE marked a turning point in the nation's history, bringing an end to the native rule of the Saite Dynasty and ushering in a period of foreign domination under the Achaemenid Persian Empire. The Twenty-seventh Dynasty, which corresponds to the First Persian Period, saw Egypt transformed from a powerful and independent civilization to a province within a vast imperial system. In this chapter, we will delve into the details of the Persian conquest and explore the key events, figures, and developments that characterized the Twenty-seventh Dynasty, shedding light on a crucial yet often overlooked period in ancient Egyptian history.

The Persian Invasion and the Fall of the Saite Dynasty

The Achaemenid Persian Empire, under the leadership of Cyrus the Great and his successors, had rapidly expanded its territories in the 6th century BCE, incorporating vast regions of the ancient Near East under its control. By the time of Cambyses II, the son of Cyrus the Great, Egypt had become an attractive target for conquest due to its strategic location, abundant resources, and weakened state following the reign of the last Saite pharaoh, Psamtik III.

In 525 BCE, Cambyses II launched a successful invasion of Egypt, capitalizing on internal divisions and a diminished military capacity. After defeating Psamtik III at the Battle of Pelusium, the Persians swiftly consolidated their control over the Nile Valley, effectively ending the rule of the Saite Dynasty and establishing the Twenty-seventh Dynasty.

Governance and Administration under the Achaemenid Persians

With Egypt now a part of the vast Achaemenid Empire, the Persian rulers sought to assert their authority and maintain control over the region through a combination of military force, administrative reforms, and cultural integration. Egypt was governed by Persian satraps, or governors, who reported directly to the Great King in Persepolis. These satraps were responsible for enforcing the empire's laws, collecting taxes, and maintaining order in their respective provinces.

The Persian administration incorporated elements of the existing Egyptian bureaucracy, relying on local scribes, priests, and officials to carry out the day-to-day affairs of the state. This approach allowed the Persians to effectively govern their new province while minimizing the risk of rebellion and unrest.

Religion and Culture during the Twenty-seventh Dynasty

Despite their foreign rule, the Achaemenid Persians generally adopted a policy of religious tolerance and cultural preservation in Egypt. Egyptian religious practices and institutions were allowed to continue, and the Persian rulers even made efforts to patronize the native gods and temples. For instance, Cambyses II is known to have made offerings to the gods Amun and Ptah, while his successor, Darius I, undertook restoration work at the Temple of Hibis in Kharga Oasis and commissioned the construction of a temple dedicated to Amun at Susa, his capital in Persia.

This policy of tolerance and respect for Egyptian religious traditions helped to secure the loyalty and cooperation of the Egyptian priesthood and the local population. However, the Persians also sought to promote their own culture and religion, as evidenced by the introduction of Persian artistic motifs, such as the winged sun disc and the "master of animals" motif, in

Egyptian art and architecture.

Resistance and Rebellion against Persian Rule

Throughout the Twenty-seventh Dynasty, there were several
instances of rebellion and resistance against Persian rule
in Egypt. These uprisings were often led by local Egyptian
leaders, who sought to exploit moments of weakness and
instability within the Persian Empire to regain their nation's
independence.

One notable example of rebellion occurred during the reign of
Darius I, when a Libyan prince named Inaros led a revolt against
the Persian satrap Aryandes in 460 BCE. Inaros was able to
seize control of a significant portion of the Nile Delta and even
managed to capture the city of Memphis. However, the rebellion
ultimately failed when the Persians, with the aid of their
Athenian allies, crushed Inaros' forces and restablished control
over Egypt.

Another significant uprising took place in 404 BCE, following
the death of the Persian king Darius II. This time, a native
Egyptian prince named Amyrtaeus was able to exploit the
power vacuum created by the Persian succession crisis and
successfully overthrow the Persian satrapy. Amyrtaeus'
victory marked the end of the Twenty-seventh Dynasty and
the beginning of the Twenty-eighth Dynasty, a brief period of
native Egyptian rule that would be followed by two more short-
lived native dynasties before the return of Persian control in the
Thirty-first Dynasty.

Economic and Social Developments under Persian Rule

The Persian conquest of Egypt had a significant impact on
the country's economy and social structure. The Achaemenid
Empire heavily taxed its provinces, and Egypt was no exception.
These taxes were used to fund the empire's military campaigns,
monumental building projects, and the lavish lifestyles of the

Persian ruling class. As a result, the Egyptian economy, which had enjoyed a period of prosperity under the Saite Dynasty, experienced a decline during the Twenty-seventh Dynasty.

Despite these challenges, the Nile Valley remained a critical source of grain for the Persian Empire, and trade between Egypt and other regions of the empire flourished. The Persians also continued to invest in infrastructure projects, such as the completion of the canal connecting the Nile to the Red Sea, which had been initiated by the Saite pharaoh Necho II. This canal facilitated trade between the Mediterranean and the Indian Ocean, further integrating Egypt into the broader Achaemenid economy.

The social structure of Egypt also evolved during the Twenty-seventh Dynasty, as Persian elites and administrators joined the ranks of the Egyptian ruling class. Intermarriage between Persians and Egyptians became more common, leading to the emergence of a new, multicultural elite that combined aspects of both Egyptian and Persian culture. This blending of cultures would have lasting effects on Egypt's artistic, linguistic, and religious traditions.


The Persian Conquest and the Twenty-seventh Dynasty represent a significant period of transformation and adaptation in ancient Egyptian history. The incorporation of Egypt into the Achaemenid Persian Empire marked the end of native rule and the beginning of a tumultuous era characterized by foreign domination, political instability, and cultural exchange.

Despite the challenges and setbacks faced by Egypt under Persian rule, the resilience and adaptability of the Egyptian people allowed their civilization to endure and evolve in the face of adversity. The Twenty-seventh Dynasty, while often overshadowed by the more famous eras of ancient Egyptian history, provides valuable insights into the complex dynamics

One of Alexander's most significant contributions to Egypt's history was the founding of the city of Alexandria in 331 BCE. Strategically located on the Mediterranean coast, Alexandria was designed to be a hub of commerce, culture, and intellectual exchange, attracting scholars, merchants, and artists from across the ancient world.

To further secure his rule and integrate Greek and Egyptian religious traditions, Alexander and his successor, Ptolemy I Soter, promoted the cult of Serapis. Serapis was a syncretic deity that combined elements of the Greek god Zeus and the Egyptian god Osiris, serving as a symbol of unity between the Greek and Egyptian populations. The cult of Serapis played a crucial role in legitimizing the Ptolemaic Dynasty and fostering cultural exchange between the diverse inhabitants of Egypt.

The Rise of the Ptolemies and the Ptolemaic Dynasty

Following Alexander's death in 323 BCE, his vast empire was divided among his generals, with Egypt falling under the control of Ptolemy I Soter. Ptolemy I, a shrewd and capable ruler, established the Ptolemaic Dynasty, which would govern Egypt for nearly three centuries.

The Ptolemies sought to consolidate their power by adopting the trappings and traditions of native Egyptian pharaohs, such as divine kingship, temple patronage, and the use of hieroglyphic inscriptions. Simultaneously, they promoted Greek language, art, and culture, creating a unique fusion of Egyptian and Hellenistic traditions that characterized the Greco-Roman Period.

Ptolemaic Egypt under Ptolemy I Soter and his successors, such as Ptolemy II Philadelphus, became a major power in the Mediterranean world, engaging in diplomacy, warfare, and cultural exchange with other Hellenistic kingdoms and the emerging Roman Republic.

The Lighthouse of Alexandria and the Library of Alexandria

The Ptolemies invested heavily in the development of Alexandria, transforming it into one of the most magnificent and influential cities of the ancient world. Two of the city's most famous landmarks, the Lighthouse of Alexandria and the Library of Alexandria, were constructed during the reign of Ptolemy II Philadelphus and stand as testament to the grandeur and intellectual prowess of the Ptolemaic era.

The Lighthouse of Alexandria, also known as the Pharos of Alexandria, was an architectural marvel and one of the Seven Wonders of the Ancient World. Standing at approximately 120 meters tall, the lighthouse was a symbol of Ptolemaic power and an essential guide for the countless ships navigating the busy harbor of Alexandria.

The Library of Alexandria, meanwhile, was the intellectual heart of the city and the ancient world. Founded by Ptolemy I Soter and expanded by Ptolemy II Philadelphus, the library aimed to collect all the knowledge of the world in one place. Scholars estimate that at its height, the Library of Alexandria housed between 400,000 and 700,000 scrolls, covering a vast array of subjects, including literature, science, mathematics, and philosophy. The library attracted some of the greatest minds of the time, such as the mathematician Euclid, the astronomer Eratosthenes, and the philosopher Plotinus, making Alexandria a vibrant center of learning and intellectual discovery.

Social and Economic Developments in Ptolemaic Egypt

Under Ptolemaic rule, the social and economic landscape of Egypt underwent significant changes. The Greek settlers and administrators formed a new ruling class, intermarrying with the native Egyptian aristocracy and adopting elements of Egyptian culture. This fusion of Greek and Egyptian customs created a multicultural society, with Greek and Egyptian languages, religion, and art coexisting side by side.

The Ptolemaic economy flourished due to the kingdom's abundant resources, strategic location, and extensive trade network. Egypt's fertile land provided grain, which was exported throughout the Mediterranean, while its mines produced valuable metals and precious stones. Alexandria's bustling harbor facilitated trade with the wider Hellenistic world and the eastern Mediterranean, bringing wealth and prosperity to the Ptolemaic Kingdom.

The arrival of Alexander the Great and the subsequent rise of the Ptolemies marked the beginning of the Greco-Roman Period in Egypt, an era defined by the fusion of Egyptian, Greek, and Roman culture and the growing influence of foreign powers. The Ptolemaic Dynasty fostered an environment of cultural exchange and intellectual development, transforming Alexandria into a beacon of learning and commerce.

Though the Ptolemaic era was not without its challenges, such as internal strife, dynastic disputes, and external threats, it remains a fascinating and vibrant chapter in Egypt's long and storied history. The Ptolemaic legacy would continue to shape the region long after the dynasty's fall, as the Roman Empire absorbed Egypt and incorporated its cultural, religious, and intellectual traditions into its vast imperial framework.

# CHAPTER 23: THE PTOLEMAIC DYNASTY - A HELLENISTIC EGYPT

The Ptolemaic Dynasty, which ruled Egypt from 305 BCE to 30 BCE, represented a unique period in the history of ancient Egypt, characterized by the fusion of Egyptian and Greek culture and the creation of a distinct Hellenistic society. This dynasty was marked by political intrigue, territorial expansion, and cultural achievements that left a lasting impact on the region. In this chapter, we will delve into the key events, personalities, and accomplishments of the Ptolemaic Dynasty, highlighting the nuances of this fascinating era and its significance in the broader context of ancient Egyptian history.

Ptolemy I Soter: Establishing the Ptolemaic Dynasty

Ptolemy I Soter, a former general of Alexander the Great, established the Ptolemaic Dynasty in 305 BCE after the death of Alexander and the division of his empire among his generals. Ptolemy I faced considerable challenges in asserting and maintaining control over Egypt, including rival claimants to the throne and potential invasions from neighboring powers. Nevertheless, Ptolemy I proved to be a skilled strategist and statesman, consolidating his rule and laying the foundations for the Hellenistic society that would flourish under his successors.

To strengthen his position, Ptolemy I adopted the traditional Egyptian practice of divine kingship, portraying himself as the successor of the native pharaohs and incorporating elements of Egyptian religion and iconography into his rule. He also founded the city of Alexandria, which would become the seat of the Ptolemaic Dynasty and a major center of commerce, learning, and culture in the Mediterranean world.

The Expansion and Rivalries of the Ptolemaic Dynasty

Under the rule of Ptolemy I Soter and his successors, Ptolemy II Philadelphus, Ptolemy III Euergetes, and Ptolemy IV Philopator, the Ptolemaic Kingdom expanded its territories, at times controlling parts of modern-day Libya, Cyprus, and the Levant. These territorial gains, however, brought the Ptolemies into conflict with their Hellenistic neighbors, particularly the Seleucid Empire and the Kingdom of Macedon.

The Ptolemies engaged in a series of wars with their rivals, known as the Syrian Wars, which spanned several generations and were fought over the control of strategically important territories in the eastern Mediterranean. The outcome of these conflicts was mixed, with both the Ptolemies and their opponents experiencing victories and defeats.

Cultural Achievements and Developments under the Ptolemies

One of the defining characteristics of the Ptolemaic Dynasty was the blending of Egyptian and Greek culture, which gave rise to a distinct Hellenistic society. Ptolemaic rulers actively patronized the arts and sciences, sponsoring the construction of magnificent buildings, such as the Library of Alexandria, the Lighthouse of Alexandria, and the Serapeum. These architectural wonders not only showcased the wealth and power of the Ptolemies, but also served as centers of learning and cultural exchange.

Under the Ptolemies, Greek and Egyptian deities were often combined, creating new syncretic gods, such as Serapis, a fusion of the Greek god Zeus and the Egyptian god Osiris. This religious syncretism helped to foster a sense of unity between the Greek and Egyptian populations, legitimizing Ptolemaic rule and facilitating the exchange of ideas and customs.

The Ptolemaic Dynasty also witnessed advancements in various fields of knowledge, including mathematics, astronomy, and medicine. Scholars such as Euclid, Eratosthenes, and Herophilus made significant contributions to their respective disciplines, and their work laid the foundation for many modern scientific principles and discoveries.

The Ptolemies encouraged the translation of Egyptian texts into Greek, making the rich literary and religious heritage of Egypt more accessible to a wider audience. This process of cultural exchange and integration, known as Hellenization, had a profound impact on the development of the arts, literature, and philosophy in the Hellenistic world.

Women and Power in the Ptolemaic Dynasty

Another notable aspect of the Ptolemaic Dynasty was the prominent role played by women in the political sphere. Ptolemaic queens, such as Arsinoe II, Berenice II, and Cleopatra VII, were not only consorts to their husbands but also influential political figures in their own right. These queens often co-ruled with their husbands or sons and were responsible for making important decisions regarding diplomacy, warfare, and domestic affairs.

Cleopatra VII, the last pharaoh of the Ptolemaic Dynasty, is perhaps the most famous of these powerful women. A skilled politician, she forged strategic alliances with Roman leaders Julius Caesar and Mark Antony, attempting to safeguard Egypt's independence and maintain her own position of power. Although ultimately unsuccessful, Cleopatra's reign was marked by a resurgence in Egyptian culture and her efforts to preserve her kingdom's autonomy in the face of Roman expansion.

Decline and Fall of the Ptolemaic Dynasty

Despite their cultural and intellectual achievements, the Ptolemaic Dynasty faced numerous challenges, including internal strife, dynastic disputes, and a weakening economy.

The power struggles within the royal family often led to periods of instability and weakened the central authority, allowing for the rise of local rebellions and the intervention of foreign powers.

As the Roman Republic grew in power and influence, Egypt became increasingly dependent on Roman support for its stability and protection. This dependency eventually led to the loss of Egyptian independence, as the Roman general Octavian (later known as Augustus) defeated Mark Antony and Cleopatra at the Battle of Actium in 31 BCE, leading to the annexation of Egypt by the Roman Empire in 30 BCE and the end of the Ptolemaic Dynasty.

The Ptolemaic Dynasty represents a unique and fascinating period in ancient Egyptian history, marked by the blending of Egyptian and Greek cultures and the creation of a Hellenistic society that left a lasting impact on the Mediterranean world. From the architectural marvels of Alexandria to the scientific and intellectual achievements of its scholars, the Ptolemaic era stands as a testament to the dynamism and adaptability of ancient Egypt in the face of changing political and cultural landscapes.

Despite the eventual decline and fall of the Ptolemaic Dynasty, the legacy of this period continues to resonate in the fields of art, literature, science, and religion. As we explore the later chapters of Egyptian history, the Hellenistic influence remains evident, demonstrating the enduring power of cultural exchange and adaptation in the face of adversity.

# CHAPTER 24: CLEOPATRA VII - THE LAST PHARAOH

Cleopatra VII, the last Pharaoh of ancient Egypt and one of the most iconic figures in history, ruled during the waning days of the Ptolemaic Dynasty. Born in 69 BCE, Cleopatra's life was marked by political intrigue, turbulent relationships, and ultimately, tragedy. Yet, her intelligence, charisma, and ambition have captured the imagination of generations, ensuring her enduring legacy in the annals of history. In this chapter, we will explore the life and times of Cleopatra VII, examining her reign, her relationships with Rome's most powerful leaders, and her role in the final chapter of Egypt's ancient civilization.

Cleopatra's Early Life and Ascension to the Throne

Cleopatra VII was the daughter of Pharaoh Ptolemy XII Auletes and an unknown mother, possibly Cleopatra V Tryphaena. As a member of the Ptolemaic Dynasty, Cleopatra grew up in the royal court of Alexandria, surrounded by wealth, power, and intrigue. She was highly educated, fluent in several languages, and well-versed in literature, philosophy, and the arts.

Upon the death of her father in 51 BCE, the 18-year-old Cleopatra ascended to the throne alongside her younger brother, Ptolemy XIII, who was only 10 years old at the time. As was customary in the Ptolemaic Dynasty, Cleopatra married her brother, but she soon found herself in a power struggle with Ptolemy XIII's advisors, who sought to control the young king and undermine her authority.

Cleopatra and Julius Caesar

In 48 BCE, Cleopatra was forced to flee Egypt after her brother's advisors turned against her. However, she was determined to reclaim her throne and saw an opportunity when Julius Caesar, the Roman general and statesman, arrived in Alexandria. Recognizing the potential advantages of an alliance with Rome, Cleopatra famously smuggled herself into Caesar's presence, wrapped in a carpet.

Cleopatra's intelligence and charm captivated Caesar, and the two quickly formed a personal and political alliance. With Caesar's support, Cleopatra was able to defeat her brother's forces and regain her position as Egypt's ruler. Their relationship also produced a son, Caesarion, whom Cleopatra claimed to be Caesar's heir.

In 46 BCE, Cleopatra traveled to Rome with Caesar, where she was received as a queen and lived in Caesar's villa. However, her presence in Rome was controversial, as many Romans disapproved of Caesar's relationship with a foreign queen. When Caesar was assassinated in 44 BCE, Cleopatra, fearing for her safety, returned to Egypt.

Cleopatra and Mark Antony

After Caesar's death, a power struggle ensued in Rome between his supporters and assassins. Eventually, Mark Antony, Caesar's loyal ally, emerged as one of the most powerful figures in Rome. Recognizing the strategic importance of Egypt and its queen, Antony summoned Cleopatra to Tarsus in 41 BCE to discuss her loyalty to Rome.

Cleopatra, ever the astute politician, recognized the opportunity to solidify her power and protect Egypt's interests by forming an alliance with Antony. Their meeting in Tarsus marked the beginning of a passionate love affair and a political alliance that would shape the course of history. Together, they had three children: Alexander Helios, Cleopatra Selene, and Ptolemy Philadelphus.

Antony and Cleopatra's relationship was not without its challenges, as Rome grew increasingly wary of Antony's ties to Egypt and his ambitions in the East. Tensions between Antony and his fellow triumvir, Octavian (later known as Augustus), escalated, ultimately leading to a declaration of war against Cleopatra in 32 BCE. This conflict, known as the Final War of the Roman Republic, would determine the fate of Egypt and its queen.

The Battle of Actium and Cleopatra's Demise

The decisive battle between the forces of Antony and Cleopatra and those of Octavian took place at Actium, a promontory in Greece, on September 2, 31 BCE. Despite their best efforts, Antony and Cleopatra's navy was defeated, and they were forced to retreat to Egypt.

With their defeat at Actium, Cleopatra and Antony's position in Egypt became increasingly precarious. Fearing capture by Octavian's forces, Antony took his own life in 30 BCE. Cleopatra, distraught over the loss of her lover and desperate to avoid capture, reportedly committed suicide by allowing an asp, a venomous snake, to bite her on August 12, 30 BCE. Her death marked the end of the Ptolemaic Dynasty and the beginning of Roman rule in Egypt.

Cleopatra's Legacy

Cleopatra VII remains one of the most enigmatic and iconic figures in history. As the last pharaoh of ancient Egypt, she represented the final chapter of a civilization that had endured for over 3,000 years. Her intelligence, political acumen, and legendary beauty have made her a subject of fascination for writers, artists, and historians throughout the centuries.

Cleopatra's reign was marked by her efforts to preserve Egypt's independence and maintain her own position of power in the face of a rapidly changing world. Though ultimately unsuccessful, her story serves as a testament to the courage, resilience, and adaptability that characterized ancient Egypt and its people.

As we reflect on the life and times of Cleopatra VII, we are reminded of the complexities of power, the fleeting nature of empires, and the indelible mark that a single individual can leave on the course of history. Her story, both tragic and inspiring, serves as a poignant reminder of the human dimensions of history and the timeless appeal of an extraordinary life.

In the chapters that follow, we will examine the impact of Roman rule on Egypt, the continued influence of Hellenistic culture, and the eventual decline of ancient Egyptian civilization. Through the lens of Cleopatra's reign and the Ptolemaic Dynasty, we gain valuable insights into the broader themes and trends that shaped Egypt's history and the Mediterranean world.

# CHAPTER 25: THE ROMAN CONQUEST AND THE END OF ANCIENT EGYPT

The Roman conquest of Egypt marked a turning point in the history of the ancient world, bringing an end to the native dynasties that had ruled the Nile Valley for millennia. With the death of Cleopatra VII and the annexation of Egypt by Rome in 30 BCE, the curtain fell on the last act of ancient Egypt's storied history. In this chapter, we will explore the impact of Roman rule on Egypt, the cultural and political changes that took place during this time, and the ultimate decline of the ancient Egyptian civilization.

Egypt under Roman Rule

Following the defeat of Cleopatra and Mark Antony at the Battle of Actium and their subsequent deaths, Egypt was formally incorporated into the Roman Empire as a province. Octavian, now known as Augustus, sought to stabilize and consolidate Roman control over the Nile Valley by implementing a series of administrative, economic, and military reforms.

Egypt held immense strategic and economic importance for Rome. The fertile Nile Valley provided a vital source of grain for the Roman Empire, while the Red Sea trade routes facilitated access to the luxury goods and exotic products of the East. To ensure the efficient exploitation of Egypt's resources, the Romans established a highly centralized administrative system, headed by a Roman prefect who oversaw the province's governance, taxation, and military affairs.

Roman rule brought significant changes to Egyptian society and culture, as the Roman elite and their customs began to permeate the Nile Valley. New cities, such as Leontopolis and

Antinoopolis, were founded, while existing urban centers like Alexandria and Memphis experienced an infusion of Roman architecture, art, and cultural practices. However, the Romans also recognized the value of maintaining Egypt's traditional institutions, and they allowed the Egyptian priesthood and temples to continue functioning, albeit under Roman oversight.

Cultural Synthesis and Continuity

Despite the profound political and social changes that accompanied Roman rule, ancient Egyptian culture and religion proved remarkably resilient. The Egyptian pantheon of gods continued to be worshipped alongside the Roman deities, and many Roman emperors embraced the role of pharaoh, adopting Egyptian royal iconography and participating in religious rituals. This cultural synthesis is evident in the art and architecture of the period, with Roman-style temples and statues often incorporating traditional Egyptian motifs and designs.

Egyptian religion and culture also exerted a powerful influence on the Roman world, as the cults of Isis, Serapis, and other Egyptian gods spread throughout the Mediterranean. The city of Alexandria, in particular, emerged as a vibrant center of intellectual and cultural exchange, where Greek, Egyptian, and Roman scholars and artists interacted and produced innovative works in fields such as philosophy, mathematics, and astronomy.

The Decline of Ancient Egyptian Civilization

While the Roman period witnessed the continuation and adaptation of many ancient Egyptian traditions, it also marked the beginning of a slow decline for the civilization that had flourished along the Nile for thousands of years. The increased demands of the Roman Empire for grain, taxes, and labor placed a heavy burden on the Egyptian population, leading to social unrest and economic hardship.

The gradual spread of Christianity in the 3rd and 4th centuries CE further eroded the foundations of ancient Egyptian religion and culture, as temples were abandoned or repurposed as churches, and the traditional gods and rituals fell into disuse. The Roman Empire itself was also facing internal and external pressures, with the provinces along the eastern Mediterranean, including Egypt, becoming increasingly vulnerable to the invasions of the Sassanian Persians and other foreign powers.

By the time of the Arab-Islamic conquest in 641 CE, the ancient Egyptian civilization had largely vanished, leaving behind only the monumental ruins and inscriptions that testified to its past glories. The Arabic language and the Islamic faith would come to dominate Egypt, supplanting the hieroglyphic script and the ancient pantheon of gods that had once defined the Nile Valley. Yet, despite these profound transformations, the legacy of ancient Egypt would continue to resonate in the collective memory and imagination of the world.

The Roman conquest of Egypt and the subsequent centuries of Roman rule marked the end of an era for the ancient Egyptian civilization. While the political and cultural landscape of the Nile Valley underwent significant changes, the resilience of the Egyptian people and their traditions ensured that their history and achievements would endure, even as the world around them evolved.

The Roman period in Egypt provides a fascinating glimpse into the complex interactions between cultures, religions, and empires in the ancient Mediterranean world. It serves as a testament to the adaptability and dynamism of the Egyptian civilization, which, over the course of its long history, had absorbed and transformed the influence of numerous foreign powers, from the Hyksos and the Nubians to the Greeks and Romans.

As we conclude our journey through the history of ancient Egypt, we are left with a sense of awe and admiration for the civilization that had flourished along the banks of the Nile for over 3,000 years. The monuments, art, and literature of ancient Egypt continue to captivate and inspire us, offering a window into a world that was both profoundly different from our own and yet strikingly familiar in its human dimensions.

The story of ancient Egypt is ultimately a story of human ingenuity, resilience, and adaptability, qualities that remain as relevant today as they were in the time of the pharaohs. By studying the history of ancient Egypt, we not only gain insights into the lives and achievements of a remarkable civilization, but we also deepen our understanding of the broader patterns and forces that have shaped the human experience across time and space.

# CHAPTER 26: THE REDISCOVERY OF ANCIENT EGYPT: NAPOLEON AND THE BIRTH OF EGYPTOLOGY

For centuries following the Arab-Islamic conquest of Egypt, the ancient civilization that had once flourished along the Nile lay largely forgotten, its monumental ruins and inscriptions an enigmatic testament to a lost world. It was not until the late 18th and early 19th centuries, with the advent of Napoleon Bonaparte's Egyptian expedition and the subsequent birth of the field of Egyptology, that the Western world began to rediscover and appreciate the extraordinary achievements of ancient Egypt. In this chapter, we will explore the events and discoveries that led to the reawakening of interest in Egypt's ancient past, the development of the scientific study of Egyptian history, and the enduring legacy of ancient Egypt in the modern world.

Napoleon's Egyptian Expedition

The French campaign in Egypt, led by Napoleon Bonaparte from 1798 to 1801, was motivated by a combination of strategic, economic, and ideological factors. Napoleon sought to undermine British influence in the eastern Mediterranean, establish a French presence in the region, and promote the ideals of the French Revolution by liberating Egypt from Ottoman rule.

However, Napoleon's expedition was not only a military campaign but also a scholarly enterprise. He was accompanied by a team of more than 150 scientists, engineers, and artists, known as the "savants," who were tasked with studying and documenting the natural, cultural, and historical aspects of Egypt. Their work laid the foundations for the modern discipline of Egyptology and sparked a renewed fascination with ancient Egypt in Europe.

The Discovery of the Rosetta Stone

One of the most significant discoveries made during Napoleon's Egyptian expedition was the Rosetta Stone, a granodiorite slab inscribed with a decree issued by Ptolemy V in 196 BCE. The decree was written in three scripts: hieroglyphic, Demotic, and Greek. The Rosetta Stone, discovered by French soldiers near the town of Rashid (Rosetta) in 1799, would prove to be the key to deciphering the ancient Egyptian hieroglyphic script and unlocking the secrets of Egypt's ancient past.

The Rosetta Stone was subsequently seized by the British as a spoil of war following Napoleon's defeat and transported to the British Museum in London, where it remains on display today. The Stone's decipherment in the early 19th century by French scholar Jean-François Champollion and British polymath Thomas Young revolutionized the study of ancient Egypt, allowing scholars to read the hieroglyphic inscriptions and texts that had remained mysterious for over a millennium.

The Birth of Egyptology

The decipherment of the Rosetta Stone and the scholarly work of Napoleon's savants marked the beginning of the systematic study of ancient Egypt and the emergence of Egyptology as a distinct academic discipline. European scholars and explorers flocked to Egypt, eager to explore, excavate, and document the ancient monuments and artifacts that had lain hidden for centuries.

Institutions dedicated to the study of Egyptology were established in major European cities, such as the Institut d'Égypte in Cairo, the École des Langues Orientales in Paris, and the Egypt Exploration Society in London. These organizations sponsored archaeological expeditions, fostered scholarly collaboration, and facilitated the dissemination of knowledge about ancient Egypt to a wider audience.

The Rediscovery of Ancient Egypt in Art and Literature

The rediscovery of ancient Egypt had a profound impact on European art, architecture, and literature during the 19th and early 20th centuries. The fascination with Egypt's ancient past inspired the Egyptomania craze, which saw the incorporation of Egyptian motifs and styles into various forms of artistic expression, such as the decorative arts, painting, and architecture. Prominent examples of this trend include the Egyptian Revival architecture, which featured obelisks, sphinxes, and other Egyptian elements in buildings and monuments across Europe and America.

In literature, the romantic allure of ancient Egypt captivated the imaginations of writers and poets, who incorporated Egyptian themes, settings, and characters into their works. Notable examples include the poems of Percy Bysshe Shelley, such as "Ozymandias," and the novels of H. Rider Haggard, such as "She" and "King Solomon's Mines." This fascination with ancient Egypt also extended to the burgeoning field of popular entertainment, with the appearance of early films and stage productions featuring Egyptian settings and storylines.

The Legacy of Ancient Egypt in the Modern World

The rediscovery of ancient Egypt and the birth of Egyptology have left an indelible mark on the modern world. The scientific study of Egypt's ancient past has contributed significantly to our understanding of human history and the development of complex societies, revealing the extraordinary achievements of the ancient Egyptians in fields such as art, architecture, science, and literature.

The story of ancient Egypt also serves as a powerful reminder of the resilience and adaptability of human civilizations in the face of change and adversity. The enduring fascination with ancient Egypt reflects the universal human desire to explore and understand our past, as well as our capacity to be inspired by the achievements and challenges of those who came before us.

In conclusion, the rediscovery of ancient Egypt, beginning with Napoleon's Egyptian expedition and continuing with the development of Egyptology as a scholarly discipline, has brought the rich history and culture of this ancient civilization back to life. The legacy of ancient Egypt continues to resonate in the modern world, providing us with a wealth of knowledge, inspiration, and wonder. As we continue to study and appreciate the achievements of the ancient Egyptians, we are reminded of the timeless power of human creativity, perseverance, and ingenuity, qualities that have shaped our past and will continue to shape our future.

# CHAPTER 27: DECIPHERING THE PAST: THE ROSETTA STONE AND THE WORK OF JEAN-FRANÇOIS CHAMPOLLION

The Rosetta Stone, discovered during Napoleon's Egyptian expedition, proved to be one of the most significant archaeological finds in history. This remarkable artifact held the key to deciphering ancient Egyptian hieroglyphs, a script that had remained a mystery for over a thousand years. The work of French scholar Jean-François Champollion played a pivotal role in unlocking the secrets of the Rosetta Stone and, by extension, the entire ancient Egyptian civilization. In this chapter, we will delve into the discovery of the Rosetta Stone, its historical significance, and the groundbreaking work of Champollion that transformed our understanding of ancient Egypt.

The Rosetta Stone: A Bilingual Decree

The Rosetta Stone is a granodiorite slab inscribed with a decree issued in 196 BCE by Ptolemy V, a Hellenistic ruler of Egypt. The decree, which commemorates the coronation of Ptolemy V, is inscribed in three scripts: hieroglyphic, Demotic, and Greek. Hieroglyphic was the formal script used by the ancient Egyptians for religious and monumental texts, while Demotic was the more common script used for everyday communication. Greek, on the other hand, was the language of the ruling Ptolemaic dynasty, which had its origins in Macedon.

The fact that the same decree was inscribed in three different scripts was crucial to the eventual decipherment of hieroglyphs. The scholars who studied the Rosetta Stone recognized that the three inscriptions contained the same text, which meant that by comparing the scripts, they could potentially unlock the meaning of the hieroglyphs.

Jean-François Champollion: The Father of Egyptology

Jean-François Champollion (1790-1832) was a French scholar and linguist whose groundbreaking work on the Rosetta Stone laid the foundations for the modern study of ancient Egypt. Born in Figeac, France, Champollion was a prodigious student who displayed a remarkable talent for languages from an early age. By the time he was a teenager, he was fluent in several ancient languages, including Greek, Hebrew, and Latin.

Champollion's interest in Egypt was ignited by the reports and publications of the savants who had accompanied Napoleon's expedition, and he devoted himself to the study of Egyptian antiquities and the decipherment of hieroglyphs. He was particularly fascinated by the Rosetta Stone and recognized its potential as a key to understanding the mysterious script.

Deciphering the Rosetta Stone

The decipherment of the Rosetta Stone was a complex and challenging task that required a deep understanding of ancient languages and scripts, as well as a keen analytical mind. Champollion began his work on the Stone by focusing on the Greek text, which was already well-understood by scholars. He then compared the Greek text to the Demotic and hieroglyphic inscriptions, searching for correlations and patterns that could reveal the meaning of the Egyptian scripts.

Champollion's breakthrough came in 1822 when he realized that the hieroglyphic script was not purely symbolic or ideographic, as many scholars had previously believed, but also included phonetic elements that represented the sounds of the ancient Egyptian language. This insight allowed him to identify the phonetic values of several hieroglyphic signs and to begin deciphering the inscriptions on the Rosetta Stone.

Champollion's work on the Rosetta Stone culminated in

the publication of his seminal work, "Précis du système hiéroglyphique des anciens Égyptiens" (Summary of the Hieroglyphic System of the Ancient Egyptians), in 1824. In this landmark publication, Champollion demonstrated the validity of his decipherment method and laid out a comprehensive system for reading and understanding hieroglyphic inscriptions. His work was met with widespread acclaim and established him as the foremost expert on ancient Egyptian language and history.

The Impact of Champollion's Work

The decipherment of the Rosetta Stone by Champollion marked a turning point in the study of ancient Egypt. With the ability to read and understand hieroglyphs, scholars could now access a wealth of previously inaccessible texts, inscriptions, and documents, shedding light on the history, religion, culture, and daily life of the ancient Egyptians.

Champollion's work also had a profound impact on the emerging field of Egyptology, which gained momentum as more scholars and explorers flocked to Egypt to study its ancient monuments and artifacts. The decipherment of hieroglyphs allowed for a more accurate dating and interpretation of these monuments, contributing to a greater understanding of the chronological development of ancient Egyptian civilization.

The Rosetta Stone and Champollion's decipherment methods also had implications for the study of other ancient scripts and civilizations. The principles and techniques developed by Champollion were subsequently applied to the decipherment of other ancient languages, such as cuneiform, which unlocked the secrets of Mesopotamian history and culture.

The Legacy of the Rosetta Stone and Champollion

Today, the Rosetta Stone and the work of Jean-François Champollion are celebrated as pivotal achievements in the history of archaeology and the study of ancient civilizations. The Rosetta Stone remains one of the most famous and iconic artifacts in the world, symbolizing the power of human curiosity and the potential for unlocking the secrets of the past.

Champollion's work continues to inspire scholars, linguists, and archaeologists, as well as generations of students and enthusiasts who are captivated by the rich history and culture of ancient Egypt. The decipherment of hieroglyphs and the birth of Egyptology have not only transformed our understanding of ancient Egypt but also deepened our appreciation for the ingenuity, creativity, and resilience of the human spirit.

In conclusion, the discovery of the Rosetta Stone and the groundbreaking work of Jean-François Champollion in deciphering its inscriptions have had a profound and lasting impact on the study of ancient Egypt and the wider field of archaeology. The legacy of the Rosetta Stone and Champollion's decipherment continues to resonate in the modern world, reminding us of the importance of preserving and understanding our shared human past and inspiring us to continue exploring the mysteries and wonders of ancient civilizations.

# CHAPTER 28: THE ONGOING MYSTERIES OF ANCIENT EGYPT

Despite the significant advances in our understanding of ancient Egypt due to the work of archaeologists, linguists, and historians, there are still many mysteries that remain unsolved. These enduring enigmas continue to captivate researchers and the public alike, sparking debates, theories, and ongoing investigations in the quest for answers. In this chapter, we will explore some of the most fascinating and puzzling mysteries of ancient Egypt, delving into the questions that keep scholars searching for answers and fuel the enduring fascination with this remarkable civilization.

The Lost Labyrinth of Egypt

The ancient Greek historian Herodotus, writing in the fifth century BCE, described a colossal, labyrinthine structure located near Lake Moeris in Egypt. According to Herodotus, this labyrinth contained thousands of rooms and chambers, as well as intricate passages and hallways that were so complex, it was nearly impossible to navigate without getting lost. The labyrinth was said to have been constructed by the Pharaoh Amenemhat III during the Middle Kingdom and was possibly a mortuary temple or a complex for religious ceremonies.

Despite extensive archaeological investigations in the region, the exact location and nature of this labyrinth remain unknown. Some scholars suggest that the labyrinth may have been destroyed or buried over time, while others believe that it may still be waiting to be discovered. The mystery of the lost labyrinth continues to intrigue researchers and fuel speculation about the purpose and fate of this enigmatic structure.

The Unknown Origins of the Sphinx

The Great Sphinx of Giza is one of the most iconic and enigmatic monuments of ancient Egypt. This colossal statue, depicting a human-headed lion, was carved from a single limestone outcrop and is thought to represent the Pharaoh Khafre, who ruled during the Fourth Dynasty of the Old Kingdom. Despite its fame, the Sphinx's origins and purpose remain the subject of ongoing debate and speculation.

Some researchers argue that the Sphinx predates the Fourth Dynasty, suggesting that it may have been built by an earlier, unknown civilization. Others propose that the Sphinx may have originally had a different head or served a different purpose than what is commonly believed. The debate surrounding the origins and meaning of the Sphinx underscores the many unanswered questions that persist about the culture and achievements of ancient Egypt.

The Disappearance of Queen Nefertiti

Queen Nefertiti, the wife of the Pharaoh Akhenaten, was one of the most powerful and influential women in ancient Egyptian history. She played a significant role in the religious revolution that occurred during her husband's reign, as they promoted the worship of the sun god Aten and sought to suppress the traditional Egyptian pantheon.

Despite her prominence, the fate of Queen Nefertiti remains a mystery. After the death of Akhenaten, Nefertiti seemingly vanished from the historical record, leaving no definitive evidence of her final resting place or the circumstances of her demise. Some scholars believe that she may have assumed the throne under a different name, while others speculate that she may have been buried in a secret tomb that has yet to be discovered. The search for clues about the life and fate of Queen Nefertiti continues to captivate researchers and the public alike, as new discoveries and theories continue to emerge.

The Mysterious Demise of the Old Kingdom

The Old Kingdom, spanning from approximately 2686 to 2181 BCE, was a period of remarkable stability, prosperity, and artistic achievement in ancient Egypt. However, this era came to an abrupt and mysterious end, as the centralized government collapsed, and the country descended into chaos during the First Intermediate Period.

The exact causes of the Old Kingdom's demise remain the subject of ongoing debate and investigation. Some scholars suggest that a combination of factors, including environmental changes, internal strife , and economic decline, may have contributed to the collapse. Others propose that external factors, such as invasions or natural disasters, may have played a role in the sudden disintegration of the Old Kingdom's political and social structures. The enduring mystery of the Old Kingdom's fall serves as a reminder of the complex and interconnected factors that can shape the course of history, and the challenges that even the most powerful civilizations can face.

The Purpose of the Pyramids

The pyramids of ancient Egypt, particularly the Great Pyramid of Giza, are among the most recognizable and enigmatic structures in human history. While it is widely accepted that these monumental tombs were built to house the remains of pharaohs and serve as a testament to their power and divinity, there is still much debate and speculation surrounding the construction methods, astronomical alignments, and symbolic significance of the pyramids.

Some researchers argue that the precise alignment of the pyramids with celestial bodies, such as stars and constellations, may reveal hidden insights into the ancient Egyptians' understanding of astronomy, mathematics, and spirituality. Others suggest that the pyramids may have served additional, yet unknown purposes beyond their function as tombs. The ongoing investigations into the mysteries of the pyramids highlight the multifaceted nature of ancient Egyptian civilization and the enduring appeal of these architectural wonders.

The ongoing mysteries of ancient Egypt serve as a testament to the depth, complexity, and richness of this remarkable civilization. While we have made significant strides in uncovering the secrets of the ancient Egyptians, there are still many questions that remain unanswered and many discoveries yet to be made. These enduring enigmas not only challenge our understanding of ancient Egypt but also inspire us to continue exploring, investigating, and seeking the truth about the past.

As the study of ancient Egypt continues to evolve, new discoveries, theories, and insights will undoubtedly shed light on these and other mysteries, deepening our appreciation for the ingenuity and resilience of the ancient Egyptians. In the meantime, the ongoing quest for answers will keep the spirit of exploration and curiosity alive, fueling our fascination with this enigmatic and captivating civilization.

# CHAPTER 29: THE LASTING INFLUENCE OF ANCIENT EGYPT IN MODERN CULTURE

The ancient civilization of Egypt has left an indelible mark on human history, and its influence can still be felt in various aspects of modern culture. From art and architecture to literature and film, the legacy of ancient Egypt continues to captivate and inspire people around the world. In this chapter, we will explore the ways in which ancient Egyptian culture has made a lasting impact on modern society, demonstrating the enduring appeal and relevance of this fascinating civilization.

Art and Architecture

The monumental structures and exquisite artistry of ancient Egypt have long inspired architects and artists worldwide. The revival of interest in Egyptian art and architecture during the 19th and 20th centuries, often referred to as "Egyptomania," led to the incorporation of Egyptian motifs and design elements in various forms of architecture, such as the construction of obelisks, sphinxes, and Egyptian-style temples.

Examples of this influence can be found in prominent structures such as the Washington Monument in the United States, Cleopatra's Needle in London, and the Luxor Hotel in Las Vegas. The fascination with ancient Egyptian art has also influenced various art movements, including Art Deco and Surrealism, as artists incorporate Egyptian symbols and themes into their work.

Literature and Film

Ancient Egyptian history and mythology have provided rich material for writers and filmmakers, who have drawn on the captivating tales and enigmatic figures of this civilization to create enduring works of fiction and cinema. From the historical novels of Christian Jacq and Wilbur Smith to the epic films of Cecil B. DeMille and Ridley Scott, the stories of ancient Egypt have captivated audiences and captured their imaginations.

One of the most enduring literary and film icons inspired by ancient Egypt is the mummy, a figure that has appeared in countless novels, films, and television shows. The mummy, often portrayed as an undead creature seeking vengeance or retribution, embodies the allure and mystery of ancient Egypt, as well as the universal themes of life, death, and the afterlife.

Fashion and Design

The distinctive clothing, jewelry, and decorative motifs of ancient Egypt have long been a source of inspiration for fashion designers and interior decorators. The elegant, flowing garments, intricate patterns, and bold colors of ancient Egyptian attire have influenced modern fashion trends and styles, as designers incorporate these elements into their collections.

The popularity of Egyptian-inspired jewelry, featuring motifs such as scarabs, lotus flowers, and the Eye of Horus, attests to the enduring appeal of ancient Egyptian design. Similarly, interior design trends often reflect a fascination with Egyptian motifs and aesthetics, as homeowners and decorators incorporate Egyptian-style furniture, artwork, and textiles into their living spaces.

Spirituality and Esotericism

The complex religious beliefs and practices of ancient Egypt have had a lasting impact on modern spirituality and esoteric thought. The ancient Egyptian pantheon, with its diverse array of gods and goddesses, has influenced various contemporary spiritual movements, including New Age practices and modern Paganism.

The concept of the afterlife, as portrayed in ancient Egyptian funerary texts and art, has also resonated with modern spiritual seekers, who find inspiration in the Egyptian understanding of death and the soul's journey. Additionally, the mystical aspects of ancient Egyptian culture, such as the use of amulets, spells, and rituals, have inspired various forms of esotericism and alternative spirituality.

The enduring influence of ancient Egypt in modern culture is a testament to the timeless appeal and significance of this remarkable civilization. From the awe-inspiring architecture and artistry to the captivating stories and spiritual traditions, the legacy of ancient Egypt continues to resonate in various aspects of our contemporary world.

As we reflect on the impact of ancient Egypt in modern culture, we are reminded of the ways in which the past continues to shape and inform our present, and the importance of preserving and understanding our shared history. The fascination with ancient Egypt also underscores the universal human desire to explore and unravel the mysteries of our ancestors, fostering a sense of connection and continuity across the ages.

Education and Science

The ancient Egyptians' contributions to the fields of mathematics, astronomy, and medicine have left a lasting impact on modern scientific thought and education. The development of the calendar, the understanding of the movement of celestial bodies, and the establishment of basic mathematical principles are all indebted to the work of ancient Egyptian scholars.

The study of ancient Egyptian medicine has also provided

valuable insights into the history of medical practice and knowledge, as researchers analyze ancient medical texts and archaeological findings to learn about the Egyptians' understanding of the human body and their treatment of various ailments.

In modern educational settings, the history and achievements of ancient Egypt often serve as a source of inspiration and fascination for students, helping to spark curiosity and interest in the study of the past. The interdisciplinary nature of Egyptology – encompassing fields such as archaeology, linguistics, and anthropology – offers a rich and diverse array of learning opportunities for those interested in exploring the history and culture of ancient Egypt.

Pop Culture and Entertainment

The allure of ancient Egypt has also made its way into the realm of pop culture and entertainment, as the themes, symbols, and stories of this civilization continue to inspire various forms of creative expression. Music, theatre, and visual arts often incorporate elements of ancient Egyptian culture, as artists and performers seek to evoke the mystery and grandeur of this fascinating civilization.

In the world of gaming, ancient Egypt has served as the backdrop for countless video games, board games, and tabletop role-playing games, providing players with immersive and engaging experiences that transport them to the world of the pharaohs, gods, and pyramids. Additionally, the popularity of Egyptian-themed escape rooms, museum exhibits, and other interactive experiences attests to the enduring fascination with ancient Egypt and the desire to explore and uncover its many secrets.

In conclusion, the lasting influence of ancient Egypt in modern culture is a testament to the power of human curiosity, creativity, and the enduring appeal of a civilization that continues to captivate and inspire. As we continue to delve into the mysteries of ancient Egypt and uncover new insights and discoveries, the legacy of this remarkable civilization will undoubtedly continue to enrich and inform our understanding of the world around us.

# CHAPTER 30: THE ART OF MUMMIFICATION

The practice of mummification, the preservation of the deceased's body for the afterlife, is one of the most enduring and fascinating aspects of ancient Egyptian culture. This intricate and time-consuming process was deeply rooted in Egyptian religious beliefs and played a crucial role in the lives of both the elite and the common people. In this chapter, we will delve into the art of mummification, examining the process itself, its significance in ancient Egypt, and the role of mummies in Egyptian society and religion.

The Process of Mummification: An In-Depth Look

Mummification in ancient Egypt was a complex and labor-intensive process that required skilled embalmers and various materials, tools, and techniques. The main goal of mummification was to preserve the deceased's body as a suitable vessel for the soul in the afterlife. The following is an overview of the essential steps in the mummification process:

Cleansing the body: The deceased's body was first washed with water from the Nile, which was considered sacred, and then cleansed with a mixture of natron and water. Natron, a naturally occurring salt, played a crucial role in the mummification process due to its desiccating and antibacterial properties.

Removal of internal organs: The embalmers removed most of the internal organs, such as the lungs, stomach, liver, and intestines, through an incision in the left side of the abdomen. These organs were then separately treated with natron, wrapped in linen, and placed in canopic jars to be buried with the deceased. The heart, considered the seat of intelligence and emotion, was left in the body, as it was believed to be essential for the afterlife.

Dehydration of the body: The body cavity was stuffed with natron, and the entire body was covered with natron for 40 days to dehydrate and preserve the flesh. After this period, the body was removed from the natron, and the remaining moisture was eliminated using linen and sawdust.

Wrapping the body: The embalmers then wrapped the body in multiple layers of linen, applying resin or gum between the layers to hold them together and provide additional preservation. During the wrapping process, amulets and other protective charms were placed within the layers to ensure the deceased's safe passage to the afterlife.

Final preparations: The wrapped body, now a mummy, was placed in a wooden or stone coffin, often accompanied by various grave goods such as jewelry, food, and furniture. A funerary mask, designed to resemble the deceased, was placed over the mummy's face, ensuring that the soul could recognize its body in the afterlife.

The Significance of Mummification in Ancient Egypt

Mummification was of paramount importance in ancient Egyptian culture, as it was believed to be a necessary step in the journey to the afterlife. The preservation of the body was essential for the soul's survival, as it provided a physical anchor for the soul to return to in the afterlife. Additionally, mummification was seen as a means of emulating the gods, particularly Osiris, the god of the afterlife, who was also believed to have been mummified.

The Role of Mummies in Egyptian Society and Religion

Mummies played a significant role in Egyptian society and religion, as they served as tangible reminders of the afterlife and the importance of proper funerary rites. Mummification was not only reserved for the pharaohs and the elite; many commoners also underwent the process, although the quality and complexity of the mummification would vary depending on the individual's social status and wealth.

Mummies also served as a focal point for religious rituals and offerings. In the tombs of the deceased, family members would regularly perform ceremonies and leave offerings of food and drink to sustain the deceased's soul in the afterlife. This ritualistic practice emphasised the strong connection between the living and the dead in ancient Egyptian society.

Moreover, the mummification process itself was deeply connected to Egyptian religious beliefs. The embalmers who conducted the mummification were considered to be skilled and sacred professionals, often associated with the god Anubis, the god of mummification and the afterlife. The rites and rituals performed during the mummification process were designed to ensure the deceased's successful transition to the afterlife and protection from any potential dangers or obstacles they might encounter.

In addition to human mummies, many animal mummies have been discovered in Egypt, indicating that animals also played a significant role in religious practices. These animals, often considered sacred, were believed to serve as intermediaries between the gods and humans. They were carefully mummified and placed in specially designed animal necropolises, where they would accompany their human counterparts in the afterlife.

The art of mummification was an essential aspect of ancient Egyptian culture, deeply rooted in religious beliefs and societal practices. The intricate process of mummification, with its numerous steps and skilled embalmers, demonstrates the immense importance placed on the preservation of the deceased's body for the afterlife. Mummies played a central role in Egyptian society and religion, serving as a powerful reminder of the connection between the living and the dead and the enduring belief in the afterlife. As we continue to explore the rich history and culture of ancient Egypt, the study of mummification provides a unique window into the complex beliefs and practices that shaped this fascinating civilization.

# CHAPTER 31: THE SCIENCE AND SECRETS OF MUMMIES

Modern scientific advancements have allowed researchers and Egyptologists to delve deeper into the mysteries of ancient Egyptian mummies, uncovering new insights into the lives, health, and customs of this remarkable civilization. In this chapter, we will explore some of the fascinating discoveries made through the study of mummies and the ways in which modern science has helped to shed light on the secrets of ancient Egypt.

Techniques for Studying Mummies

In the past, the study of mummies often involved invasive and destructive methods, such as unwrapping the mummies or conducting autopsies, which resulted in the loss of valuable information and the potential damage to the mummies themselves. Today, however, researchers employ a variety of non-invasive techniques to study mummies, allowing for a more comprehensive and accurate understanding of these ancient remains.

X-ray and CT scans: These imaging techniques allow researchers to see inside the mummies without disturbing their wrappings or causing damage to the remains. By analyzing the skeletal structures and any artifacts contained within the wrappings, researchers can gather information on the mummies' age, sex, health, and burial customs.

DNA analysis: Advances in genetic research have enabled scientists to extract and analyze DNA from mummies, providing insights into the ancestry, familial relationships, and population dynamics of ancient Egyptians. DNA analysis has also helped to identify certain genetic diseases and conditions that may have affected the ancient population.

Chemical and isotopic analysis: By examining the chemical composition of mummies' teeth, bones, and hair, researchers can gather information about the individuals' diet, health, and geographical origin. This information can offer valuable insights into the daily lives and cultural practices of ancient Egyptians.

Discoveries and Insights from Mummy Studies

The study of mummies has led to numerous fascinating discoveries and insights into the lives of ancient Egyptians:

Health and disease: The examination of mummies has provided valuable information on the health of the ancient Egyptian population. Common health issues, such as dental problems, arthritis, and parasitic infections, have been identified through the study of mummy remains. Additionally, researchers have discovered evidence of more serious diseases, such as tuberculosis and cancer, among some mummies, providing a better understanding of the prevalence and impact of these conditions in ancient Egypt.

Lifestyle and occupation: The analysis of mummies has shed light on the lifestyles and occupations of the individuals. For example, skeletal wear and tear can indicate the type of work performed by the deceased, while the presence of certain materials or artifacts within the wrappings can offer clues to their social status and occupation.

Artistic and cultural practices: The study of mummies has also provided insights into ancient Egyptian artistic and cultural practices. Intricate funerary masks, amulets, and jewelry discovered within mummy wrappings reflect the skill and craftsmanship of ancient Egyptian artisans, as well as the beliefs and customs of the time.

Mummification techniques: The examination of mummies has allowed researchers to better understand the various methods and techniques employed in the mummification process, as well as how these practices evolved over time. This knowledge not only enhances our understanding of ancient Egyptian religious beliefs but also helps to preserve and protect existing mummies for future generations.

The study of mummies has greatly enriched our understanding of ancient Egyptian civilization, providing a unique and intimate glimpse into the lives, health, and customs of this remarkable society. As modern science continues to advance and new techniques for studying mummies are developed, the secrets of these ancient remains will undoubtedly continue to reveal the rich and complex tapestry of ancient Egyptian history and culture.

# CHAPTER 32: THE GODS OF ANCIENT EGYPT

The Pantheon of Gods and Goddesses: An Overview

Ancient Egyptian religion encompassed a vast and diverse pantheon of gods and goddesses, each of whom played a crucial role in the lives of the Egyptian people. With deities representing every aspect of existence, from the natural world to human emotions, the pantheon of gods and goddesses is a testament to the profound spirituality and rich complexity of ancient Egyptian culture. In this chapter, we will provide an overview of some of the most significant gods and goddesses in the Egyptian pantheon, exploring their roles, attributes, and the ways in which they were worshipped by the ancient Egyptians.

Major Gods and Goddesses

Amun-Ra: Amun-Ra was the supreme god of the Egyptian pantheon, formed by the fusion of Amun, the god of Thebes and the hidden power, and Ra, the sun god. Amun-Ra was considered the king of the gods, and his worship was central to Egyptian religion. He was associated with creation, the sun, and fertility, and was often depicted as a man with a headdress featuring a solar disk and two tall plumes.

Osiris: Osiris was the god of the afterlife, resurrection, and fertility. He was the first pharaoh of Egypt who was killed and resurrected by his sister-wife Isis, becoming the ruler of the underworld. Osiris was usually depicted as a green-skinned man with a pharaoh's beard, wearing the atef crown and holding the crook and flail, symbols of his divine authority.

Isis: Isis was the goddess of motherhood, magic, and healing, and the devoted wife of Osiris. She played a crucial role in the resurrection of her husband, and her protective and nurturing qualities made her a popular deity among the Egyptian people. Isis was often depicted as a woman wearing a headdress featuring a throne or a solar disk with cow horns, symbolizing her role as a divine queen and mother.

Horus: Horus, the son of Isis and Osiris, was the god of the sky, kingship, and protection. As the rightful heir to his father's throne, he battled his uncle Seth to avenge his father's death and establish his reign as the divine king of Egypt. Horus was commonly depicted as a falcon or as a man with a falcon head, wearing the double crown of Upper and Lower Egypt.

Seth: Seth was the god of chaos, storms, and disorder. He was the brother and rival of Osiris, whom he murdered in an attempt to usurp the throne of Egypt. Although Seth was associated with negative qualities, he was also considered a powerful and important deity, responsible for maintaining the balance between order and chaos. Seth was typically depicted as a man with the head of a mysterious, dog-like creature known as the Set animal.

Hathor: Hathor was the goddess of love, beauty, music, and motherhood. She was often associated with the sky and the sun, and was considered the divine mother of the pharaohs. Hathor was commonly depicted as a cow or a woman with cow ears, or as a woman wearing a headdress featuring a solar disk and cow horns.

Thoth: Thoth was the god of wisdom, writing, and the moon. He was considered the scribe and record-keeper of the gods and was believed to have invented writing and language. Thoth was often depicted as a man with the head of an ibis or as a baboon, holding a writing palette and stylus.

Anubis: Anubis was the god of mummification, the afterlife, and the protection of tombs. He played a crucial role in the funerary rites of the ancient Egyptians, guiding the souls of the deceased through the underworld and ensuring their safe passage to the afterlife. Anubis was commonly depicted as a man with the head of a jackal or as a jackal, often seen presiding over tombs or accompanying the deceased in funerary scenes.

Maat: Maat was the goddess of truth, justice, and order. She represented the fundamental principles of balance and harmony upon which the universe was founded. Maat played a crucial role in the judgment of the dead, as their hearts were weighed against her feather to determine their fate in the afterlife. Maat was typically depicted as a woman with an ostrich feather on her head, symbolizing truth and justice.

Ptah: Ptah was the god of craftsmen, architects, and creation. He was considered the divine patron of artisans and the creator of the world through his thoughts and words. Ptah was often depicted as a mummiform man wearing a skullcap, holding a scepter composed of the ankh, was, and djed symbols, representing life, power, and stability.

Worship and Rituals

The gods and goddesses of the Egyptian pantheon were honored and worshipped through a variety of rituals, ceremonies, and festivals. Temples dedicated to specific deities were constructed throughout Egypt, and daily offerings were made to the gods in the form of food, drink, and incense. Priests and priestesses served as intermediaries between the people and the gods, performing rituals and maintaining the sanctity of the temples.

In addition to daily rituals, many gods and goddesses were celebrated through annual festivals, which were significant social and religious events in ancient Egyptian society. These festivals often involved processions, music, and feasting, as well as the reenactment of myths and sacred ceremonies to honor and appease the gods.

The pantheon of gods and goddesses in ancient Egypt represents a complex and diverse array of divine forces that shaped every aspect of life for the Egyptian people. The worship of these deities was a central aspect of ancient Egyptian culture, reflecting the deep spirituality and rich cosmology that formed the foundation of their civilization. By understanding the roles and attributes of the major gods and goddesses, we can gain valuable insights into the beliefs, values, and worldview of the ancient Egyptians.

# CHAPTER 33: THE IMPORTANCE OF RELIGION IN ANCIENT EGYPTIAN SOCIETY

Religion was a fundamental aspect of ancient Egyptian society, deeply ingrained in every facet of daily life, from politics and economics to art and architecture. It provided the Egyptian people with a sense of stability, continuity, and purpose, while also serving as a powerful unifying force that shaped the development of their civilization for over three millennia. In this chapter, we will explore the central role of religion in ancient Egyptian society, examining the ways in which it influenced the lives of the people, the structure of the state, and the expression of their unique cultural identity.

The Role of Religion in Everyday Life

For the ancient Egyptians, religion was not a separate sphere of life but rather an all-encompassing worldview that permeated every aspect of their existence. They believed that the world was inhabited by a multitude of gods and goddesses who controlled the forces of nature, determined the course of human events, and communicated with the people through dreams, omens, and divine oracles.

This belief in the active presence of the divine led the Egyptians to integrate religious rituals and practices into their daily lives. They offered prayers, amulets, and small statues as tokens of devotion to their favorite deities, seeking protection, guidance, and blessings in their personal affairs. They also observed various religious festivals throughout the year, which provided opportunities for communal celebration, worship, and the reaffirmation of social bonds.

## Religion and the State

The close relationship between religion and the state was a defining characteristic of ancient Egyptian civilization. The pharaoh was not only the political leader of Egypt but also the embodiment of divine power, serving as the intermediary between the gods and the people. As the "Son of Ra," the pharaoh was responsible for maintaining the cosmic order of Maat, which involved ensuring the prosperity of the land, upholding justice, and performing the necessary religious rituals to appease the gods.

The priesthood played a crucial role in supporting the pharaoh's divine authority and managing the religious affairs of the state. Priests and priestesses served as custodians of the temples, where they conducted daily rituals, administered offerings, and interpreted the will of the gods. They also played a significant role in the education of the elite, passing on the sacred knowledge and religious traditions that underpinned the social hierarchy.

## Religion and Art

The profound influence of religion on ancient Egyptian art is evident in the vast array of temples, tombs, and monuments dedicated to the gods and the pharaohs, who were considered divine beings themselves. These architectural masterpieces were not only expressions of religious devotion but also symbols of the state's power and prestige, designed to reinforce the divine authority of the pharaoh and the sacred order of the cosmos.

Similarly, the art of ancient Egypt – including sculpture, painting, and relief – was deeply imbued with religious symbolism and meaning. The depiction of gods, goddesses, and mythological scenes served not only as artistic decoration but also as a means of communicating the core beliefs and values of the society. The strict adherence to artistic conventions and the use of highly stylized, symbolic imagery were intended to convey the eternal, unchanging nature of the divine realm and its manifestations in the world of the living.

The importance of religion in ancient Egyptian society cannot be overstated, as it shaped every aspect of their lives, from their personal relationships to the organization of the state and the creation of their most enduring cultural achievements. The centrality of religion in Egyptian civilization highlights the crucial role that spirituality played in the development of human societies throughout history, offering valuable insights into the ways in which people have sought to understand and engage with the divine forces that govern their existence.

# CHAPTER 34: THE ROLE OF PRIESTS AND PRIESTESSES IN EGYPTIAN RELIGION

In ancient Egyptian society, priests and priestesses played a vital role in maintaining the delicate balance between the divine and the mortal realms. They served as the intermediaries between the people and the gods, ensuring that the proper rituals were performed, and the divine order was upheld. In this chapter, we will delve into the role of priests and priestesses in Egyptian religion, examining their duties, responsibilities, and the impact they had on the spiritual and social life of the Egyptian people.

The Hierarchy of the Priesthood

The priesthood in ancient Egypt was a complex and hierarchical institution, with various levels of authority and specialization. At the top of the hierarchy were the high priests, who held the most prestigious and powerful positions within the religious hierarchy. High priests were often associated with specific temples or deities and acted as the chief administrators of their respective temples.

Beneath the high priests were the priests and priestesses, who carried out the day-to-day rituals and duties within the temples. They were responsible for tending to the cult statues of the gods, performing daily rituals, and managing the offerings made by the people. There were also specialized roles within the priesthood, such as lector priests who were responsible for reciting religious texts during ceremonies and rituals, and wab priests who were responsible for maintaining the temple's ritual purity.

In addition to these roles, there were numerous other religious officials, including temple scribes, musicians, and artisans, all of whom played a part in the functioning of the religious institutions.

Duties and Responsibilities of Priests and Priestesses

The primary responsibility of priests and priestesses was to maintain the connection between the gods and the people. To achieve this, they performed a variety of religious rituals and ceremonies within the temples. One of the most important daily rituals was the opening of the sanctuary, during which the cult statue of the god would be cleansed, dressed, and adorned with offerings. This ritual was believed to reawaken the god and ensure their continued presence and favor.

Priests and priestesses also played a crucial role in the festivals and processions that punctuated the Egyptian religious calendar. These events were essential for reaffirming the community's connection to the gods and ensuring the continued prosperity of the land. During these ceremonies, priests and priestesses would carry the cult statue of the god through the streets, enabling the people to witness and participate in the divine presence.

In addition to their religious duties, priests and priestesses were responsible for the administration and upkeep of the temples. This included overseeing the agricultural estates that provided the temples with their income, managing the distribution of offerings, and supervising the various temple workers and craftsmen.

The Role of Priests and Priestesses in Society

As religious leaders and intermediaries between the gods and the people, priests and priestesses held a prominent position in ancient Egyptian society. Their association with the divine granted them a level of prestige and respect that set them apart from the rest of the population. They were often exempt from certain taxes and obligations and enjoyed a higher standard of living than most other Egyptians.

Furthermore, the priesthood played a significant role in the education of the elite, as they were the keepers of the sacred knowledge and religious traditions. The sons of high-ranking officials and nobles were often trained as priests, ensuring that the religious and political elite remained closely connected.

The role of priests and priestesses in ancient Egyptian religion was both complex and multifaceted, reflecting the central importance of religion in the lives of the Egyptian people. Through their dedication to the gods and their service to the temples, the priests and priestesses maintained the divine order and preserved the spiritual foundations of Egyptian society. Their influence extended far beyond the religious sphere, shaping the social, political, and cultural landscape of ancient Egypt in profound and enduring ways.

In their capacity as religious leaders, educators, and administrators, priests and priestesses played a crucial role in maintaining the continuity of Egypt's religious traditions and ensuring the smooth functioning of its temples and religious institutions. Their intimate knowledge of the sacred texts, rituals, and ceremonies allowed them to transmit the accumulated wisdom of their civilization to future generations, thereby preserving the essence of Egyptian culture and identity.

Furthermore, the priests and priestesses served as role models for the Egyptian people, embodying the values of piety, devotion, and service to the gods that were so central to their worldview. By dedicating their lives to the divine, they reinforced the pervasive belief in the interconnectedness of the spiritual and the material realms, which was the foundation of Egyptian religion and society.

In sum, the role of priests and priestesses in Egyptian religion highlights the profound significance of religious institutions and practices in shaping the development of human civilizations throughout history. By examining the duties, responsibilities, and social impact of these religious figures, we can gain a deeper understanding of the spiritual dimensions of ancient Egyptian culture and the ways in which religion served as a driving force behind the remarkable achievements of this enduring civilization.

# CHAPTER 35: THE EVOLUTION OF PYRAMID BUILDING IN ANCIENT EGYPT

The pyramids of ancient Egypt are among the most recognizable and awe-inspiring structures in human history. These architectural marvels have captivated the imagination of people for thousands of years and remain a testament to the ingenuity, creativity, and ambition of the ancient Egyptians. In this chapter, we will trace the evolution of pyramid building in ancient Egypt, exploring the various stages of their development and the innovations that shaped their design and construction.

The Early Dynastic Period: The Step Pyramid of Djoser

The origins of pyramid building can be traced back to the Early Dynastic Period, specifically to the reign of Pharaoh Djoser in the 27th century BCE. Djoser's step pyramid, designed by the architect Imhotep, represents a significant innovation in tomb architecture and laid the foundation for the development of the true pyramids.

The Step Pyramid of Djoser, located at Saqqara, was initially conceived as a mastaba, a flat-roofed, rectangular tomb structure common during this period. However, Imhotep's innovative design involved stacking six increasingly smaller mastabas on top of one another, creating a step-like structure that reached a height of approximately 62 meters. This architectural breakthrough marked the beginning of the pyramid-building tradition in ancient Egypt.

The Old Kingdom: The Age of the Great Pyramids

The Old Kingdom, spanning from the 27th to the 22nd century

BCE, is often referred to as the "Age of the Pyramids," as this period saw the construction of some of the most iconic and ambitious pyramids in Egyptian history. The architectural innovations of the Step Pyramid laid the groundwork for the development of the true pyramid, characterized by its smooth, triangular sides that meet at a single point at the top.

The most famous pyramids of this period are the Giza pyramids, built during the Fourth Dynasty for Pharaohs Khufu, Khafre, and Menkaure. The largest of these, the Great Pyramid of Khufu, stands at an impressive 147 meters in height, making it the tallest structure in the world for over 3,800 years. The construction of these massive monuments required vast amounts of labor, resources, and organization, reflecting the immense power and wealth of the Old Kingdom pharaohs.

In addition to the Giza pyramids, the Old Kingdom saw the construction of many other pyramids, such as the Red Pyramid and the Bent Pyramid of Sneferu, which represent significant advancements in pyramid-building techniques.

The Middle Kingdom: A Resurgence of Pyramid Building

Following the collapse of the Old Kingdom and the subsequent First Intermediate Period, the Middle Kingdom marked a resurgence of pyramid building in ancient Egypt. While the pyramids of this period were smaller and less elaborate than their Old Kingdom predecessors, they still represented a continuation of the tradition and an affirmation of the pharaohs' divine status.

Notable pyramids from the Middle Kingdom include the Pyramid of Amenemhat I at Lisht and the Pyramid of Senusret I at El-Lahun. These pyramids featured innovative construction techniques, such as using mudbrick cores encased in limestone, which allowed for a more efficient use of resources.

The New Kingdom and Beyond: The Decline of Pyramid

Building

The New Kingdom, which began in the 16th century BCE, marked a shift away from the construction of pyramids as royal tombs. Instead, pharaohs of this period favored hidden rock-cut tombs in the Valley of the Kings, such as the famous tomb of Tutankhamun. This shift was likely due to concerns about tomb security, as the prominent pyramids had become targets for tomb robbers.

Despite the decline in pyramid building, the tradition continued on a smaller scale during the Late Period and the Ptolemaic era, with smaller pyramids and pyramid-like structures being constructed for both religious and funerary purposes. These later pyramids, however, never reached the grandeur and scale of their Old and Middle Kingdom predecessors.

The evolution of pyramid building in ancient Egypt is a fascinating journey that highlights the ingenuity, ambition, and cultural significance of these architectural masterpieces. From the innovative step pyramid of Djoser to the awe-inspiring Great Pyramid of Khufu, the pyramids of Egypt have captivated the world for millennia and continue to stand as a testament to the remarkable achievements of the ancient Egyptians.

As we explore the history and development of these iconic structures, we gain a deeper understanding of the religious, political, and social forces that shaped the course of ancient Egyptian civilization. The pyramids, in their various forms and stages of development, provide a window into the rich tapestry of Egyptian history and offer a unique perspective on the power and resilience of this enduring culture.

# CHAPTER 36: THE CONSTRUCTION AND DESIGN OF THE GREAT PYRAMIDS OF GIZA

The Great Pyramids of Giza, consisting of the pyramids of Khufu, Khafre, and Menkaure, stand as some of the most remarkable and enduring achievements of human civilization. Their construction and design reflect not only the advanced architectural and engineering skills of the ancient Egyptians, but also their deep spiritual and cultural beliefs. In this chapter, we will delve into the construction and design of the Great Pyramids of Giza, exploring the techniques and innovations that made these wonders of the ancient world possible, as well as the broader context in which they were built.

Construction Techniques and Materials

One of the most intriguing aspects of the Great Pyramids is the sheer scale and complexity of their construction. The precise techniques used to build these massive structures remain a subject of debate among scholars, but it is generally agreed that they involved a combination of skilled labor, vast resources, and innovative engineering methods.

The primary building material for the pyramids was limestone, quarried from nearby sites and transported to Giza using the Nile River and a network of canals. Large stone blocks, weighing several tons each, were cut from the quarries and transported to the construction site, where they were carefully arranged and fitted together to form the pyramid's core.

The construction process likely involved the use of ramps to transport and position the massive stone blocks. There are several theories regarding the design and use of these ramps, with some suggesting a straight ramp leading directly up to the pyramid, while others propose a spiral ramp that encircled the structure as it was built.

Design and Architectural Innovations

The design of the Great Pyramids was based on the principle of the "squared circle," which sought to create a perfect balance between the earthbound square base and the celestial, circular apex. This concept was deeply rooted in ancient Egyptian religious beliefs, which viewed the pharaoh as a bridge between the earthly and divine realms.

The pyramids of Giza feature several design innovations and refinements that distinguish them from earlier pyramid structures. For example, the Great Pyramid of Khufu has a unique internal layout, featuring ascending and descending passages, the Grand Gallery, and three main chambers: the King's Chamber, the Queen's Chamber, and the unfinished Subterranean Chamber. The pyramid's design also incorporates ventilation shafts and advanced structural techniques, such as relieving chambers above the King's Chamber, to help distribute the weight of the massive stone blocks.

The pyramids of Khafre and Menkaure, while smaller than the Great Pyramid, also exhibit sophisticated design elements and construction techniques. Both pyramids feature internal chambers and passageways, and the Pyramid of Khafre is known for its distinctive casing of polished Tura limestone, which would have given the structure a smooth, gleaming appearance when it was first built.

The Broader Context: Religion, Culture, and Power

The construction and design of the Great Pyramids of Giza cannot be fully understood without considering the broader cultural, religious, and political context in which they were built. The pyramids served as monumental tombs for the pharaohs, reflecting their divine status and the central role of the afterlife in ancient Egyptian beliefs. They also functioned as powerful symbols of the pharaoh's authority and the might of the Egyptian state, showcasing the wealth, resources, and technological prowess of the civilization.

The Great Pyramids of Giza stand as a testament to the ingenuity, ambition, and spiritual depth of the ancient Egyptians. By examining their construction and design, we can gain valuable insights into the complex interplay of religion, culture, and power that shaped the development of this remarkable civilization. As we continue to explore the mysteries and marvels of ancient Egypt, the Great Pyramids of Giza will undoubtedly remain a source of fascination and inspiration for generations to come.

In the millennia since their construction, the Great Pyramids have captivated the imagination of people around the world, becoming iconic symbols of human achievement and the enigmatic nature of ancient history. The knowledge and skills employed in their creation continue to inspire awe and respect, even as modern technology continues to unlock new secrets and understanding about their construction, function, and significance.

As we delve deeper into the study of the Great Pyramids and their role in ancient Egyptian society, we are reminded of the profound impact that these structures have had on our understanding of history, architecture, and the human spirit. The Great Pyramids of Giza serve as a lasting testament to the creativity, determination, and vision of the ancient Egyptians, whose achievements continue to influence and inspire us today.

# CHAPTER 37: GEOMETRY AND ASTRONOMY IN ANCIENT EGYPT

The Use of Geometry in Ancient Egyptian Architecture and Art
Introduction

Geometry and astronomy played crucial roles in the development of ancient Egyptian architecture and art, reflecting the civilization's advanced understanding of mathematical principles and celestial phenomena. In this chapter, we will explore the use of geometry in ancient Egyptian architecture and art, examining the ways in which the Egyptians employed mathematical concepts to create harmonious, aesthetically pleasing, and functional designs that continue to inspire and captivate the imagination of people around the world.

Geometry in Architecture: The Golden Ratio and the Principle of Proportion

One of the most significant ways in which geometry was incorporated into ancient Egyptian architecture is through the use of the Golden Ratio and the principle of proportion. The Golden Ratio, also known as Phi (approximately 1.618), is a mathematical constant that can be found throughout nature, art, and architecture, and was known to the ancient Egyptians as the "sacred ratio."

The Egyptians used the Golden Ratio to create harmonious proportions in their architectural designs, including the layout of temples, palaces, and the iconic pyramids. This principle of proportion was essential to the aesthetic appeal and functionality of these structures, ensuring that they were both visually pleasing and structurally sound.

In addition to the Golden Ratio, the ancient Egyptians also employed a system of grids and standardized units of measurement to ensure consistency and harmony in their architectural designs. This systematic approach to architecture allowed for the precise alignment of buildings with celestial bodies, further illustrating the connection between geometry, astronomy, and ancient Egyptian culture.

Geometry in Art: The Canon of Proportions and the Representation of the Human Form

The use of geometry in ancient Egyptian art can be seen most prominently in the representation of the human form, which adhered to a strict set of guidelines known as the Canon of Proportions. The Canon of Proportions was a system of idealized measurements that dictated the proper proportions and dimensions of the human body in Egyptian art, ensuring that figures were depicted consistently and according to established aesthetic principles.

This adherence to the Canon of Proportions can be seen in the depiction of both royal and non-royal figures in Egyptian art, from the intricate wall reliefs found in tombs and temples to the statues and sculptures that adorned public spaces. The use of geometry in the representation of the human form allowed for the creation of stylized, yet harmonious, depictions that were both visually pleasing and symbolic of the divine nature of the pharaohs and the gods.

Astronomy and Geometry: The Celestial Connection

The ancient Egyptians were keen observers of the night sky, and their understanding of astronomy played a significant role in the development of their architectural and artistic practices. Many Egyptian structures, including temples and the pyramids, were designed with precise alignments to celestial bodies such as the sun, moon, and stars, reflecting the civilization's belief in the connection between the heavens and the earth.

This celestial connection can also be seen in the use of astronomical symbols and motifs in Egyptian art, which often incorporated representations of the sun, moon, stars, and various deities associated with the heavens. The integration of astronomical knowledge and geometric principles in ancient Egyptian architecture and art highlights the civilization's advanced understanding of the natural world and its commitment to creating harmonious and meaningful designs.

Geometry and astronomy were integral aspects of ancient Egyptian culture, playing a pivotal role in the development of the civilization's architectural and artistic practices. Through the use of the Golden Ratio, the Canon of Proportions, and a deep understanding of celestial phenomena, the ancient Egyptians created enduring masterpieces of architecture and art that continue to captivate and inspire people around the world. The legacy of ancient Egyptian geometry and astronomy serves as a testament to the civilization's intellectual prowess and its profound appreciation for the beauty and harmony found in both the natural and the constructed world.

As we have explored throughout this chapter, the ancient Egyptians' mastery of geometry and their understanding of astronomy allowed them to create architectural marvels, such as the pyramids, temples, and palaces, which have withstood the test of time. Their adherence to the Canon of Proportions in art ensured the consistent and harmonious representation of the human form, reflecting their belief in the divine nature of the pharaohs and the gods.

The celestial connection present in ancient Egyptian architecture and art also demonstrates the civilization's belief in the interconnectedness of the heavens and the earth, a belief that was deeply ingrained in their religion, society, and culture. By aligning their structures with celestial bodies and incorporating astronomical symbols and motifs into their art, the ancient Egyptians sought to establish a connection with the divine and to express their understanding of the cosmos.

In conclusion, the use of geometry and astronomy in ancient Egyptian architecture and art showcases the civilization's advanced knowledge, creativity, and ability to create lasting monuments that reflect their unique cultural identity. The lasting influence of ancient Egyptian geometry and astronomy can still be seen in modern architecture, art, and design, serving as a reminder of the timeless appeal and significance of these ancient principles.

As we move forward through this book, we will continue to explore the myriad ways in which the ancient Egyptian civilization has left an indelible mark on human history, inspiring generations with their ingenuity, artistry, and profound understanding of the world around them.

# CHAPTER 38: THE DEVELOPMENT OF ASTRONOMY IN ANCIENT EGYPT

Astronomy was an integral aspect of ancient Egyptian culture, playing a significant role in religion, architecture, agriculture, and timekeeping. The development of astronomy in ancient Egypt was fueled by the civilization's fascination with the celestial world and its desire to understand the mysteries of the universe. In this chapter, we will delve into the evolution of astronomy in ancient Egypt, exploring the methods, techniques, and discoveries that shaped the civilization's understanding of the cosmos and its place within it.

Observing the Heavens: The Origins of Egyptian Astronomy

The origins of Egyptian astronomy can be traced back to the Predynastic Period (circa 6000-3100 BCE) when early Egyptians began observing and recording the movements of celestial bodies. The Nile River's annual flooding, which was crucial to agriculture, was closely linked to the heliacal rising of the star Sirius, known as Sothis in ancient Egypt. This astronomical event marked the beginning of the Egyptian New Year and signaled the onset of the inundation. This reliance on the Nile's flood cycle prompted the ancient Egyptians to closely observe the heavens and develop an understanding of the celestial patterns and their relationship to earthly events.

The Astronomical Ceilings and Star Clocks

Egyptian astronomers created detailed star maps and charts to document their observations and improve their understanding of the cosmos. Many of these maps can be found on the ceilings of tombs and temples, serving both an educational and religious purpose. The astronomical ceilings, such as those found in the tombs of Senenmut and Seti I, often featured depictions of constellations, planets, and other celestial bodies, as well as associated deities and mythological figures.

One of the most significant innovations in Egyptian astronomy was the development of star clocks, which allowed the ancient Egyptians to measure time using the movements of the stars. The oldest known star clock dates back to the Middle Kingdom (circa 2055-1650 BCE) and was found in the tomb of the vizier Senedjemib Inti. Star clocks were used to divide the night into hours and to determine the time of year based on the positions of specific stars and constellations.

The Decanal System and the Egyptian Calendar

The decanal system was a key aspect of Egyptian astronomy, in which the night sky was divided into 36 decans, each representing a 10-day period. These decans were used to create a 360-day calendar, with an additional five days added at the end of the year, known as the "epagomenal days," to make up a complete 365-day year. This calendar was widely used in ancient Egypt for administrative and religious purposes and was later adopted by other civilizations.

Astronomy and Religion: The Celestial Pantheon

Astronomy and religion were closely intertwined in ancient Egyptian culture, with the movements of celestial bodies often being associated with the actions of gods and goddesses. Many Egyptian deities were connected to celestial phenomena, such as the sun god Ra, who was believed to traverse the sky in his solar boat, and the goddess Nut, who was thought to represent the night sky, her body arching over the earth.

These celestial deities played a crucial role in the daily lives of ancient Egyptians, as their actions were believed to influence events on earth. Observing and understanding celestial phenomena were essential to maintaining the balance between the natural and divine worlds, and priests and astronomers were tasked with interpreting the significance of celestial events and the messages of the gods.

The development of astronomy in ancient Egypt was a complex and multifaceted process, driven by the civilization's curiosity, practical needs, and religious beliefs. From the origins of celestial observation to the creation of intricate star maps and the development of the Egyptian calendar, ancient Egypt's advancements in astronomy left a lasting impact on human history and our understanding of the cosmos. The celestial pantheon and the intertwining of astronomy and religion reveal the deeply ingrained connection between the natural and divine worlds in ancient Egyptian culture.

The achievements of ancient Egyptian astronomers in observing, recording, and interpreting celestial phenomena laid the foundation for later astronomical developments in other cultures, such as the Greeks and the Romans. The ancient Egyptians' deep understanding of the cosmos and their ability to integrate this knowledge into their daily lives, religion, and architecture are a testament to the ingenuity and intellectual capacity of this remarkable civilization.

As we continue our journey through the history and legacy of ancient Egypt, we will further explore the many ways in which this civilization has shaped our understanding of the world, from their impressive architectural marvels to their profound religious beliefs and the intricate art that adorned their tombs and temples. The development of astronomy in ancient Egypt serves as a reminder of the enduring fascination with the heavens that has captivated human imagination for millennia and the boundless potential for discovery that lies in the stars.

# CHAPTER 39: THE SIGNIFICANCE OF ASTRONOMY IN EGYPTIAN RELIGION AND CULTURE

Astronomy played a pivotal role in the religious, cultural, and daily life of ancient Egyptians. This enduring fascination with celestial phenomena shaped various aspects of Egyptian society, from religion and mythology to agriculture and architecture. In this chapter, we will delve deeper into the significance of astronomy in ancient Egyptian religion and culture, exploring the multifaceted ways in which the celestial world shaped the lives and beliefs of this remarkable civilization.

Cosmic Deities and Celestial Mythology

The ancient Egyptian pantheon included a wide array of gods and goddesses associated with celestial phenomena. The sun god Ra, the most prominent among them, symbolized the life-giving force of the sun and was believed to travel across the sky each day in his solar boat. At night, Ra's journey continued through the treacherous underworld, where he would battle the forces of chaos and darkness, led by the serpent deity Apophis, before being reborn each morning.

The sky goddess Nut, depicted as an arching female figure covered in stars, represented the night sky and was believed to swallow the sun each evening and give birth to it anew each morning. Other celestial deities included Thoth, the moon god associated with wisdom and writing, and Hathor, who was linked to the planet Venus and represented love, beauty, and motherhood.

These celestial deities and their mythological narratives

were deeply ingrained in Egyptian religious beliefs and practices, underscoring the importance of the cosmos in their understanding of the divine world.

## Astronomy and the Afterlife

The ancient Egyptians believed that the soul journeyed to the afterlife, and celestial phenomena were often associated with this journey. The stars, in particular, were believed to be the resting place of the souls of the deceased, and the process of mummification was thought to ensure the deceased's safe passage through the celestial realm.

The pyramids, with their precise alignment to celestial bodies, were built as eternal resting places for pharaohs, allowing them to ascend to the heavens and join the gods in the afterlife. The Pyramid Texts, inscribed on the walls of Old Kingdom pyramids, contain numerous references to stars and celestial phenomena, further highlighting the connection between astronomy and the concept of the afterlife.

## Astronomy in Daily Life and Agriculture

The ancient Egyptians relied on astronomical observations to regulate various aspects of their daily life, such as timekeeping and agriculture. The heliacal rising of Sirius (Sothis) marked the beginning of the inundation season, which was crucial for agriculture, as it brought fertile silt to the Nile Valley. The Egyptian calendar was based on the movements of celestial bodies, with the year divided into three seasons: Inundation (Akhet), Emergence (Peret), and Harvest (Shemu).

## Astronomy in Architecture and Art

The influence of astronomy on ancient Egyptian architecture and art is evident in the alignment of temples and monuments with celestial events, such as the solstices and equinoxes. The temple of Karnak, dedicated to the god Amun-Ra, features a unique alignment that allows the sun's rays to illuminate the inner sanctum during the winter solstice.

Astronomical imagery also pervaded Egyptian art, as seen in the depictions of celestial deities and celestial events on tomb and temple walls. The Dendera Zodiac, a beautifully carved bas-relief from the ceiling of the Temple of Hathor, is a prime example of the integration of astronomy into Egyptian art.

The significance of astronomy in ancient Egyptian religion and culture is a testament to the civilization's deep-rooted fascination with the cosmos and its desire to understand the mysteries of the universe. Through their observations and understanding of celestial phenomena the ancient Egyptians developed a complex religious and cultural framework that integrated the cosmos into various aspects of their daily life. From the construction of monumental pyramids and temples aligned with celestial events to the development of a calendar based on the movements of celestial bodies, the ancient Egyptians harnessed the knowledge of the heavens to shape their understanding of the world around them.

This enduring fascination with the celestial world not only shaped ancient Egyptian religion and mythology but also influenced their art, architecture, and agricultural practices. As we continue to explore the rich history and legacy of ancient Egypt, it is essential to recognize the profound impact that astronomy had on the lives and beliefs of this remarkable civilization.

The study of astronomy in ancient Egypt offers valuable insights into the intellectual pursuits and achievements of one of the most influential civilizations in human history. By uncovering the ways in which the cosmos influenced the religious, cultural, and daily life of the ancient Egyptians, we can gain a deeper understanding of the complexities of their society and the remarkable ingenuity and resilience that defined this ancient civilization.

# CHAPTER 40: DISCOVERIES IN ANCIENT EGYPT - THE DISCOVERY OF KING TUTANKHAMUN'S TOMB

Throughout our exploration of ancient Egypt's rich history and legacy, we have delved into various aspects of this remarkable civilization, including its art, architecture, religion, and astronomical achievements. In this next part of our journey, we will turn our attention to some of the most significant discoveries in the field of Egyptology, beginning with the discovery of King Tutankhamun's tomb. This remarkable find not only shed light on the life and reign of the young pharaoh but also offered valuable insights into the burial customs and funerary practices of ancient Egypt.

The Discovery of the Tomb

On November 4, 1922, British archaeologist Howard Carter and his team made one of the most significant discoveries in the history of Egyptology - the tomb of the young Pharaoh Tutankhamun in the Valley of the Kings. The tomb, designated KV62, was found almost entirely intact, a rarity among the tombs in the area, which had been extensively plundered over the centuries.

Upon entering the tomb, Carter and his team were astounded by the sheer amount of treasures and artifacts that filled the chambers. The tomb contained over 5,000 objects, including the famous golden death mask of the young king, intricately crafted furniture, jewelry, and the well-preserved mummy of Tutankhamun himself.

The Life and Reign of King Tutankhamun

Tutankhamun, also known as the "Boy King," ascended to the throne at the age of nine or ten and ruled during the 18th Dynasty (around 1334 - 1325 BCE). His reign was relatively short, as he died at the age of 19, and his rule marked a brief return to the traditional religious practices of Egypt after the tumultuous reign of his father, the monotheistic Pharaoh Akhenaten. The discovery of Tutankhamun's tomb and the wealth of information it provided about his life and reign has made him one of the most well-known and enigmatic figures in ancient Egyptian history.

The Impact of the Discovery on Egyptology

The discovery of King Tutankhamun's tomb had a profound and lasting impact on the field of Egyptology. As one of the few tombs found largely intact, it offered a unique window into the funerary practices and material culture of ancient Egypt. The artifacts discovered within the tomb have allowed researchers to better understand the daily life, beliefs, and artistic achievements of the civilization, as well as the intricacies of their burial customs.

Moreover, the worldwide fascination with the tomb and its treasures sparked a renewed interest in ancient Egypt and its history, contributing to the burgeoning field of Egyptology and inspiring generations of archaeologists, historians, and enthusiasts alike.

As we continue our exploration of ancient Egypt's lasting influence and legacy, the discovery of King Tutankhamun's tomb stands out as a pivotal moment in the field of Egyptology. The wealth of information and artifacts gleaned from this remarkable find has provided invaluable insights into the life and reign of the young pharaoh and the wider cultural, religious, and artistic landscape of ancient Egypt.

By examining the discoveries of the past, such as the tomb

of Tutankhamun, we can gain a deeper understanding of the complexities and achievements of ancient Egypt, shedding light on the enduring legacy of this influential civilization and its impact on our modern society.

The discovery of King Tutankhamun's tomb sparked widespread interest in ancient Egypt, leading to further research and excavation efforts in the region. This renewed focus on Egyptology brought to light many more fascinating details about the Boy King and the era he lived in.

## The Treasures of Tutankhamun's Tomb

Among the treasures found in Tutankhamun's tomb were numerous pieces of exquisitely crafted jewelry, such as rings, necklaces, and bracelets. These pieces were made of gold and inlaid with precious and semi-precious stones such as lapis lazuli, carnelian, and turquoise. Many of these items were not only ornamental but also carried religious and symbolic significance, reflecting the beliefs and customs of ancient Egyptian society.

One of the most iconic items discovered in the tomb was Tutankhamun's golden burial mask. This stunning piece, crafted from solid gold and adorned with lapis lazuli, quartz, and other precious stones, was placed directly over the mummy's head to represent the eternal, divine nature of the pharaoh.

Another significant artifact was a beautifully crafted alabaster chalice, known as the "Wishing Cup," inscribed with the wish that Tutankhamun "may spend millions of years...and may (he) see all the joy that is in the sun's presence." This chalice, like many other objects found in the tomb, held both practical and symbolic significance.

## Funerary Practices and the Afterlife

The tomb's contents provided valuable insights into the

funerary practices of ancient Egypt, specifically the 18th Dynasty. The Egyptians believed in the concept of an afterlife, and they considered the preservation of the body through mummification essential for the deceased to enter the afterlife successfully.

The tomb of Tutankhamun contained multiple chambers, with each room serving a specific purpose. The burial chamber housed the pharaoh's sarcophagus, while other chambers contained items intended to accompany the king into the afterlife. These items included food, wine, clothing, and even board games, reflecting the belief that the deceased would require these items in their journey through the afterlife.

The Curse of Tutankhamun's Tomb

Shortly after the discovery of the tomb, rumors of a curse began to circulate. This was fueled by a series of unfortunate events and tragedies that befell some members of Howard Carter's team and others who had entered the tomb. Although there is no concrete evidence to support the existence of a curse, the idea captured the public's imagination and contributed to the intrigue surrounding the tomb and its treasures.

The discovery of King Tutankhamun's tomb remains one of the most significant moments in the history of archaeology and Egyptology. The vast array of treasures and artifacts found within the tomb has provided scholars and historians with invaluable insights into the life and times of the young pharaoh and the ancient Egyptian civilization as a whole. This incredible find has not only deepened our understanding of this remarkable civilization, but it has also inspired generations to explore the mysteries and wonders of the past.

# CHAPTER 41: THE ROSETTA STONE AND THE DECIPHERING OF HIEROGLYPHICS

The Rosetta Stone, discovered in 1799, is a crucial artifact in the history of archaeology and linguistics. This enigmatic stone slab was the key to unlocking the mysteries of ancient Egyptian hieroglyphics, a writing system that had remained undeciphered for centuries. In this chapter, we will delve deeper into the story of the Rosetta Stone, the process of deciphering hieroglyphics, and the impact of this groundbreaking discovery on our understanding of ancient Egyptian history and culture.

The Discovery of the Rosetta Stone

The Rosetta Stone was discovered by French soldiers during Napoleon Bonaparte's military campaign in Egypt. The stone slab, which dates back to 196 BCE, was found near the town of Rashid (Rosetta) in the Nile Delta region. Measuring approximately 45 inches in height, 28.5 inches in width, and 11 inches in thickness, the Rosetta Stone is a fragment of a larger stele inscribed with a decree issued by King Ptolemy V.

What makes the Rosetta Stone remarkable is that the decree is inscribed in three different scripts: hieroglyphics, the script used by the priests and for religious texts; Demotic, a simplified form of hieroglyphics used for everyday writing; and Greek, the language of the Ptolemaic administration. This unique combination of scripts provided scholars with a crucial tool for deciphering ancient Egyptian hieroglyphics.

The Deciphering of Hieroglyphics

For centuries, the knowledge of how to read hieroglyphics had been lost, and the mysterious symbols remained indecipherable. The Rosetta Stone's trilingual inscription offered scholars a unique opportunity to unravel the secrets of this ancient writing system. The fact that the same decree was inscribed in both Greek and hieroglyphics enabled scholars to use the known Greek language as a basis for understanding the hieroglyphic script.

The task of deciphering hieroglyphics was a painstaking process that required years of dedicated research and scholarship. The breakthrough came in 1822 when French scholar Jean-François Champollion announced that he had successfully deciphered the hieroglyphic script. Champollion's work built upon the earlier efforts of scholars like Thomas Young, an English polymath who had made significant progress in identifying some of the hieroglyphic characters and their phonetic values.

Champollion's method involved comparing the names of Greek and Egyptian rulers mentioned in the inscriptions, isolating the hieroglyphic characters that corresponded to specific phonetic sounds. By analyzing the patterns and structure of the hieroglyphic script, Champollion was able to identify the phonetic values of numerous hieroglyphic characters and ultimately decipher the ancient Egyptian writing system.

The Impact of Deciphering Hieroglyphics

The deciphering of hieroglyphics had a profound impact on the study of ancient Egyptian history, culture, and religion. With the ability to read and understand hieroglyphic texts, scholars could now access a wealth of previously inaccessible information about the lives and beliefs of the ancient Egyptians.

This newfound understanding of hieroglyphics led to an explosion of interest in Egyptology and the study of ancient Egyptian civilization. Scholars were able to interpret a vast array of inscriptions on monuments, tombs, temples, and artifacts, shedding light on the history, beliefs, and everyday lives of the people who had created these remarkable works.

The discovery of the Rosetta Stone and the deciphering of hieroglyphics represent one of the most significant achievements in the history of archaeology and linguistics. The work of scholars like Jean-François Champollion not only unlocked the secrets of an ancient writing system but also opened the doors to a deeper understanding of a fascinating civilization that had been shrouded in mystery for centuries.

The impact of this discovery cannot be overstated. It revolutionized the field of Egyptology and provided a renewed sense of awe and appreciation for the rich culture, artistic achievements, and complex belief systems of the ancient Egyptians. The Rosetta Stone and the deciphering of hieroglyphics have allowed scholars to delve into the world of pharaohs, priests, and everyday people, reconstructing the narrative of a civilization that continues to captivate our imagination.

Today, the Rosetta Stone stands as a testament to the power of human curiosity, determination, and ingenuity. It reminds us of the importance of preserving and studying our shared cultural heritage and the potential rewards that await when we unravel the mysteries of the past. As we continue to explore the wonders of ancient Egypt and uncover new discoveries, the legacy of the Rosetta Stone and the deciphering of hieroglyphics will continue to inspire and inform our quest for knowledge.

# CHAPTER 42: THE UNCOVERING OF THE TOMB OF HATSHEPSUT

Hatshepsut, one of ancient Egypt's most powerful and successful pharaohs, was a woman who defied convention and reigned over a prosperous and stable kingdom during the Eighteenth Dynasty. Despite her significant achievements, her memory was nearly erased from history, and her tomb remained hidden for millennia. In this chapter, we will delve into the discovery of Hatshepsut's tomb, the challenges faced by archaeologists, and the insights this remarkable find has offered into the life and reign of this enigmatic ruler.

The Quest for Hatshepsut's Tomb

Hatshepsut's tomb had long been sought by archaeologists and Egyptologists due to her unique position in Egyptian history. Despite the systematic attempts to erase her memory, evidence of her reign persisted, and her accomplishments were too significant to be entirely forgotten. The search for her tomb gained momentum in the late 19th and early 20th centuries, as archaeologists began to piece together the fragments of her story and sought to uncover her final resting place.

The Discovery

The breakthrough came in 1903 when British archaeologist Howard Carter, who would later become famous for discovering Tutankhamun's tomb, found a series of tombs in the Valley of the Kings known as KV60. Initially, the significance of the discovery was not fully recognized, as the tombs appeared to have been looted and contained little more than a few mummified geese and some broken pottery.

However, in 1920, the American Egyptologist Herbert Winlock

examined the tomb more closely and found a sealed side chamber containing two mummies, one of which would later be identified as Hatshepsut's wet nurse, Sitre-In. This discovery led to renewed interest in the tomb, and further investigations eventually revealed that the second mummy was none other than Hatshepsut herself.

Identifying Hatshepsut

The identification of Hatshepsut's mummy was a complex and challenging process. Her tomb had been disturbed, and many of the artifacts that might have offered clues to her identity were missing or damaged. Moreover, her mummy was not found in a sarcophagus bearing her name, making it difficult to determine her identity with certainty.

A major breakthrough occurred when the archaeologist Zahi Hawass and his team used modern forensic techniques to examine the mummies found in KV60. By studying the distinctive features of Hatshepsut's teeth and comparing them to a loose tooth found in a small wooden box inscribed with her name, the team was able to confirm that one of the mummies was indeed Hatshepsut.

The Importance of Hatshepsut's Tomb

The discovery of Hatshepsut's tomb has provided invaluable insights into the life and reign of this powerful female pharaoh. Her tomb is not only a testament to her determination to be remembered and honored as a ruler, but also a reflection of her status as a key figure in ancient Egyptian history.

As we continue to study and uncover the secrets of Hatshepsut's tomb, we gain a deeper understanding of her accomplishments, her motivations, and the challenges she faced as a woman ruling in a male-dominated society. The uncovering of Hatshepsut's tomb serves as an enduring reminder of the resilience and strength of this remarkable ruler, whose legacy continues to inspire and captivate us today.

# CHAPTER 43: EGYPTIAN MEDICINE AND SCIENCE

The Advancements of Ancient Egyptian Medicine

The ancient Egyptians were pioneers in various fields, and their contributions to medicine were groundbreaking for their time. As one of the earliest civilizations to develop a structured medical system, their knowledge and understanding of the human body, diseases, and treatments laid the foundation for modern medicine. In this chapter, we will explore the advancements of ancient Egyptian medicine, highlighting their discoveries, practices, and the role of physicians in society.

Understanding the Human Body

Egyptians had a surprisingly sophisticated understanding of the human body, which can be attributed to their careful study of anatomy during the process of mummification. They identified and named various organs, understood the circulatory system, and documented the symptoms and treatments of various ailments. Some of the earliest known medical texts, such as the Edwin Smith Papyrus and the Ebers Papyrus, contain detailed descriptions of medical practices, surgical procedures, and remedies.

Medical Practices and Treatments

The ancient Egyptians employed a combination of practical treatments and spiritual healing in their approach to medicine. They used a wide range of natural remedies, including herbs, spices, minerals, and animal products, to treat various ailments. Many of these remedies are still used today in traditional and alternative medicine.

In addition to their knowledge of natural remedies, the ancient

Egyptians also practiced surgery. Some surgical procedures, such as stitching wounds and setting broken bones, were quite advanced for their time. They also used prosthetics, as evidenced by the discovery of artificial toes and other prosthetic devices in ancient tombs.

Physicians and their Role in Society

In ancient Egypt, physicians were highly respected members of society, and their skills were often passed down through generations within a family. Some physicians specialized in specific areas, such as dentistry, ophthalmology, or gynecology, while others served as general practitioners. They were employed by temples, the royal court, or the military, and were also available to treat the general population.

Physicians were expected to adhere to a strict code of ethics, which included confidentiality, honesty, and the responsibility to do no harm to their patients. Many ancient Egyptian doctors were also priests, which further emphasized the connection between medicine and religion in their society.

The Legacy of Ancient Egyptian Medicine

The advancements of ancient Egyptian medicine had a significant impact on the development of medical knowledge in other civilizations. The Greeks, for example, were heavily influenced by Egyptian medicine and adopted many of their practices and theories. Through the works of scholars such as Herodotus and Galen, the knowledge of Egyptian medicine spread throughout the ancient world and contributed to the foundations of modern medical science.

In conclusion, the ancient Egyptians made remarkable strides in the field of medicine, with their understanding of anatomy, development of medical treatments, and the role of physicians in society. Their contributions have had a lasting impact on the field of medicine and continue to be a source of fascination and inspiration for researchers and medical professionals alike.

# CHAPTER 44: THE IMPORTANCE OF SCIENCE AND TECHNOLOGY IN ANCIENT EGYPT

Ancient Egypt is renowned for its incredible feats of architecture, art, and engineering. Behind these achievements was a foundation of scientific knowledge and technological innovation that allowed the Egyptians to create their magnificent monuments and develop a thriving, advanced society. In this chapter, we will delve into the importance of science and technology in ancient Egypt, exploring their advancements in various fields and their impact on the everyday lives of the people.

## Astronomy and Timekeeping

Astronomy played a crucial role in ancient Egyptian society. The Egyptians meticulously observed the stars and other celestial bodies, developing an accurate calendar system based on the movements of the sun, moon, and stars. This understanding of the cosmos allowed them to predict the annual flooding of the Nile, which was essential for agriculture and the overall stability of the civilization.

In addition to their calendar, the Egyptians developed sundials and water clocks to measure time. These innovations were vital for organizing daily activities, religious rituals, and large-scale construction projects.

## Mathematics and Geometry

The ancient Egyptians had a deep understanding of mathematics and geometry, which was essential for the construction of their monumental structures, such as the pyramids and temples. They used sophisticated methods to calculate the dimensions, angles, and proportions required for these impressive edifices. Egyptian mathematicians also developed techniques for solving problems related to fractions, multiplication, and division, and their knowledge of geometry was instrumental in surveying land and calculating areas and volumes.

Medicine and Pharmacology

As we explored in Chapter 46, the ancient Egyptians made significant advancements in the field of medicine. They developed a vast pharmacopeia of natural remedies, documented numerous medical conditions, and devised various surgical procedures. Their understanding of the human body and its functions was impressive for their time, and their medical knowledge greatly influenced the development of medicine in other cultures.

Engineering and Architecture

The ancient Egyptians are perhaps best known for their awe-inspiring architectural feats, such as the Great Pyramid of Giza, the temples of Luxor and Karnak, and the rock-cut tombs in the Valley of the Kings. These magnificent structures were made possible by their expertise in engineering and their mastery of construction techniques. They developed methods for quarrying and transporting massive stone blocks, as well as skills in masonry, carpentry, and metalworking.

Agriculture and Irrigation

Agriculture was the backbone of the ancient Egyptian economy, and their advancements in agricultural technology were essential for sustaining their civilization. They devised intricate irrigation systems, using canals and dikes to control the flow of water from the Nile, ensuring that their crops were adequately watered throughout the growing season. They also developed tools and techniques for plowing, planting, and harvesting, which increased the efficiency and productivity of their agricultural endeavors.

In conclusion, science and technology were indispensable in ancient Egypt, shaping every aspect of their society and culture. Their achievements in astronomy, mathematics, medicine, engineering, and agriculture continue to inspire and inform modern scientific endeavors, attesting to the lasting legacy of ancient Egyptian innovation and ingenuity.

# CHAPTER 45: WOMEN IN ANCIENT EGYPT - THE ROLE OF WOMEN IN ANCIENT EGYPTIAN SOCIETY

The role of women in ancient Egyptian society was unique compared to other ancient civilizations, as they enjoyed a relatively high degree of equality and independence. Women played significant roles in various aspects of society, including family life, religion, and even governance. In this chapter, we will explore the multifaceted roles and contributions of women in ancient Egypt, highlighting their remarkable achievements and the respect they commanded in this ancient civilization.

Family Life and Marriage

Women in ancient Egypt held crucial roles in family life. They were primarily responsible for raising children, managing the household, and ensuring the well-being of the family. Marriage in ancient Egypt was considered a partnership, with both men and women having equal rights and responsibilities within the relationship.

Egyptian women had the right to own property and engage in trade, and they could also inherit and bequeath wealth. In cases of divorce, women were entitled to a fair share of the marital property and could initiate the divorce process if they felt mistreated or unhappy in the marriage.

Religion and Priesthood

Religion played a central role in ancient Egyptian society, and women held prominent positions in the religious sphere. Many of the most important deities in the Egyptian pantheon were female, including Isis, Hathor, and Nut. These goddesses represented various aspects of nature, fertility, and motherhood, and were revered by both men and women.

Women could also serve as priestesses in the temples dedicated to these goddesses, performing rituals and ceremonies to honor the gods. Some women even held the prestigious title of "God's Wife," a high-ranking religious role that brought with it considerable influence and authority.

Education and Scribes

Although formal education was primarily reserved for boys, some women in ancient Egypt had the opportunity to learn reading, writing, and arithmetic. These educated women often came from elite families and could become scribes, a highly respected profession in ancient Egypt. Female scribes were employed in various sectors, including administration, commerce, and religious institutions.

Queens and Female Rulers

Ancient Egyptian society recognized and celebrated the power and influence of its queens and female rulers. Queens were considered the earthly embodiment of goddesses, such as Isis and Hathor, and played crucial roles in supporting their husbands and ensuring the stability of the kingdom. Several queens, such as Nefertiti and Nefertari, left lasting legacies in art, architecture, and diplomacy.

Egypt also witnessed a few instances of female pharaohs who ruled in their own right, such as Hatshepsut and Cleopatra VII. These women defied gender norms and expectations to lead their people, make significant contributions to Egyptian history, and leave indelible marks on the world.

In conclusion, women in ancient Egypt held significant roles in various aspects of society, enjoying a level of freedom and equality that was uncommon in the ancient world. They contributed immensely to the development and prosperity of ancient Egypt, and their stories offer valuable insights into the rich and diverse culture of this remarkable civilization.

# CHAPTER 46: THE ACHIEVEMENTS OF FEMALE RULERS AND LEADERS IN ANCIENT EGYPT

Throughout its history, ancient Egypt saw several powerful and influential female rulers and leaders who played significant roles in the development and prosperity of the civilization. These women defied societal norms and expectations, making their mark in the realms of governance, diplomacy, religion, and culture. In this chapter, we will delve into the lives and accomplishments of some of the most prominent female rulers and leaders in ancient Egypt, celebrating their lasting legacies.

Hatshepsut
Hatshepsut, the fifth pharaoh of the Eighteenth Dynasty, is one of the most famous female rulers in ancient Egypt. She ruled for approximately 20 years (c. 1478-1458 BCE), and her reign was marked by peace, prosperity, and impressive building projects.

Hatshepsut commissioned numerous monumental constructions, such as the Temple of Deir el-Bahari, which showcased her architectural prowess and vision. She also focused on trade and diplomacy, sending expeditions to the Land of Punt (modern-day Somalia) to acquire valuable goods like incense, ebony, and gold.

Nefertiti
Nefertiti, the wife of Pharaoh Akhenaten, was a prominent figure during the Eighteenth Dynasty. Although she was not a ruler in her own right, her influence and involvement in religious and political affairs were significant.

Nefertiti was a key supporter of her husband's religious revolution, which replaced the traditional worship of multiple gods with the exclusive worship of the sun god Aten. She is also believed to have played a role in diplomacy, as letters from the Amarna Period suggest her involvement in corresponding with foreign leaders.

Cleopatra VII
Cleopatra VII, the last pharaoh of ancient Egypt, is renowned for her intelligence, beauty, and political acumen. Ruling from 51-30 BCE, she skillfully navigated the complex web of diplomacy and alliances to maintain her kingdom's independence.

Cleopatra forged strategic relationships with Roman leaders Julius Caesar and Mark Antony, which allowed her to protect and expand her realm. She was also a patron of the arts and sciences, promoting Alexandria as a center of learning and culture.

Sobekneferu
Sobekneferu was a female pharaoh of the Twelfth Dynasty, ruling for a brief period (c. 1806-1802 BCE). Although her reign was short, she is recognized as the first confirmed female pharaoh in Egyptian history. Little is known about her achievements, but her rule serves as a testament to the possibility of female leadership in ancient Egypt.

Merneith
Merneith, a queen of the First Dynasty (c. 2950 BCE), is believed to have ruled as a regent for her young son Den. She was responsible for making important decisions on behalf of the kingdom, and her tomb in Abydos demonstrates her high status and influence during her lifetime.

These remarkable women defied gender expectations and made significant contributions to the development and prosperity of ancient Egypt. Their achievements in governance, diplomacy, religion, and culture continue to inspire and inform our understanding of this fascinating civilization. By examining their legacies, we gain valuable insights into the role and importance of female rulers and leaders in ancient Egyptian society.

# CHAPTER 47: ART AND LITERATURE IN ANCIENT EGYPT

The Evolution of Egyptian Art and Sculpture

Art and sculpture played a significant role in ancient Egyptian culture, reflecting the society's values, beliefs, and traditions. Over the course of its history, Egyptian art evolved and adapted to new influences and tastes while maintaining its unique and instantly recognizable style. In this chapter, we will explore the development of Egyptian art and sculpture and their significance in ancient Egyptian society.

a. Early Dynastic Period

During the Early Dynastic Period (c. 3100-2686 BCE), the foundations of Egyptian art and sculpture were laid. Artisans began to develop a unique visual language characterized by the use of hieroglyphs, a grid system for proportion and scale, and the conventions of frontalism and profile view in depicting figures. Early examples of sculpture include the Narmer Palette, which commemorates the unification of Upper and Lower Egypt, and the statues of the pharaoh Djoser.

b. Old Kingdom

The Old Kingdom (c. 2686-2181 BCE) was a golden age for Egyptian art and sculpture. The pyramids and their associated mortuary complexes served as a canvas for artistic expression, with elaborate wall reliefs and painted scenes depicting everyday life, religious rituals, and the afterlife. Sculpture also flourished during this period, with artisans creating lifelike statues of pharaohs, nobles, and officials in stone, wood, and bronze.

c. Middle Kingdom

The Middle Kingdom (c. 2055-1650 BCE) saw a shift in artistic focus from the grandiose projects of the Old Kingdom to more intimate and personal works. Sculpture became more naturalistic and expressive, with increased attention to detail in facial features and clothing. The art of the Middle Kingdom also saw the introduction of new materials, such as faience, a glazed ceramic used to create vibrant and colorful jewelry, amulets, and figurines.

d. New Kingdom

The New Kingdom (c. 1550-1070 BCE) marked a resurgence in monumental art and sculpture, as pharaohs like Hatshepsut, Akhenaten, and Ramses II embarked on ambitious building projects. Wall reliefs and paintings became more detailed and dynamic, often depicting large-scale military campaigns and religious festivals. The Amarna Period, during the reign of Akhenaten, brought a brief but radical shift in artistic style, characterized by more fluid and expressive forms, as well as an emphasis on the royal family.

e. Late Period and Ptolemaic Era

The Late Period (c. 664-332 BCE) and the Ptolemaic Era (c. 332-30 BCE) saw the influence of foreign cultures, particularly Persian and Greek, on Egyptian art and sculpture. While traditional Egyptian styles and motifs persisted, new elements such as Greco-Roman clothing, hairstyles, and poses were incorporated, resulting in a unique fusion of artistic traditions.

Throughout its history, ancient Egyptian art and sculpture served as a powerful means of communication and expression. By examining the evolution of these art forms, we gain valuable insights into the beliefs, values, and aspirations of the civilization, as well as the artistic and cultural exchanges that shaped its development. The enduring legacy of Egyptian art and sculpture continues to captivate and inspire, offering a window into the rich and complex world of ancient Egypt.

# CHAPTER 48: THE IMPORTANCE OF LITERATURE IN ANCIENT EGYPT

In addition to the captivating art and sculpture that defined ancient Egyptian culture, literature played a significant role in shaping the society and preserving its history. The written word held immense power and prestige, and literary works encompassed various genres, including religious texts, historical accounts, poetry, and stories. In this chapter, we will delve into the importance of literature in ancient Egypt and the various forms it took.

The Origins of Egyptian Literature
Egyptian literature traces its roots to the invention of writing during the Early Dynastic Period (c. 3100-2686 BCE) with the development of hieroglyphs. These intricate pictorial symbols allowed the ancient Egyptians to record their history, religious beliefs, and daily life. Over time, the script evolved to include hieratic and demotic scripts, which were more accessible for everyday use.

Religious Texts
Religion was deeply ingrained in ancient Egyptian culture, and much of its literature focused on religious themes. The Pyramid Texts, dating back to the Old Kingdom (c. 2686-2181 BCE), are the oldest known religious texts in Egypt. These inscriptions adorned the walls of the burial chambers within the pyramids and were intended to guide the deceased pharaoh through the afterlife. Later, the Coffin Texts and the Book of the Dead provided similar guidance for the common people, with spells and instructions for navigating the afterlife.

Historical Accounts
Historical accounts were another vital aspect of Egyptian

literature. The Palermo Stone, dating back to the Old Kingdom, chronicled a list of pharaohs and their achievements, serving as a valuable resource for understanding the early history of Egypt. Other historical texts, such as the annals of Thutmose III and the inscriptions of Ramesses II, detailed military campaigns, conquests, and building projects undertaken by the pharaohs.

## Poetry and Love Songs

Poetry was a popular form of literature in ancient Egypt, with themes ranging from love and relationships to the beauty of nature. Love songs, in particular, were a unique genre that showcased the emotions and desires of the ancient Egyptians. These lyrical compositions often featured vivid imagery, metaphors, and wordplay, expressing the sentiments of the heart in a captivating and relatable manner.

## Stories and Tales

Ancient Egyptian literature also included stories and tales that conveyed moral lessons, entertained, and provided glimpses into daily life. The Tale of the Shipwrecked Sailor and the Tale of the Eloquent Peasant are two examples of such narratives that combined adventure, drama, and wisdom to engage the reader. These stories often featured fantastical elements and allegory, serving as cautionary tales or vehicles for imparting ethical guidance.

## Wisdom Literature

Wisdom literature, a prominent genre in ancient Egypt, offered advice and guidance on various aspects of life, such as family, relationships, and career. Works like The Maxims of Ptahhotep and The Instruction of Amenemope provided practical wisdom and moral teachings, often through the voice of a wise elder or a father addressing his son.

Egyptian literature was instrumental in shaping and preserving the civilization's cultural identity. Through the various genres of religious texts, historical accounts, poetry, stories, and wisdom literature, we gain a deeper understanding of the ancient Egyptian mindset and the values they held dear. The richness and diversity of ancient Egyptian literature continue to captivate and inspire, offering a unique window into the lives and hearts of this extraordinary civilization.

# CHAPTER 49: ANCIENT EGYPTIAN MYTHS AND LEGENDS

The Creation Myth: The Story of Ra and Osiris
The ancient Egyptians had a rich and vibrant mythology, filled with gods, goddesses, and a multitude of stories that explained the world around them. Central to their beliefs was the creation myth – a complex narrative that detailed the birth of the universe, the gods, and all of creation. In this chapter, we will explore the captivating story of Ra, the sun god, and Osiris, the god of the afterlife, and their roles in the Egyptian creation myth.

The story begins in the primordial waters of Nun, a vast, chaotic expanse that existed before the world came into being. Within these waters, the first divine being, the self-created god Atum, emerged. Atum was both male and female, representing the duality of creation, and from him, the first divine couple was born: Shu, the god of air, and Tefnut, the goddess of moisture. Shu and Tefnut, in turn, gave birth to Geb, the god of earth, and Nut, the goddess of the sky.

In the early days of creation, Geb and Nut were inseparable, locked together in an eternal embrace. Shu, however, intervened and lifted Nut above the earth, separating the lovers and creating the space in which the world could exist. From their union, four divine siblings were born: Osiris, Isis, Seth, and Nephthys.

Osiris, the eldest, became the king of Egypt, bringing civilization, agriculture, and the rule of law to the land. He married his sister, Isis, the goddess of fertility and magic, and together they ruled the kingdom with wisdom and benevolence.

Seth, the god of chaos and destruction, was envious of his

brother's success and hatched a devious plan to usurp the throne. He tricked Osiris into climbing into a beautiful, ornate chest, which he then sealed and cast into the Nile. Isis, heartbroken and determined to find her husband, searched tirelessly for the chest, eventually discovering it in a distant land.

But Seth was not finished with his treachery. He found the chest containing Osiris's body, dismembered it, and scattered the pieces throughout Egypt. Undeterred, Isis and her sister Nephthys, who was married to Seth, set out to gather the pieces of Osiris's body. With the help of the god Anubis, they reassembled the body and performed the first mummification, allowing Osiris to live on in the afterlife as the ruler and judge of the dead.

During her search for Osiris's body, Isis had conceived a son, Horus, who grew up in secret, protected from Seth's wrath. When he came of age, Horus challenged Seth for the throne of Egypt, leading to a series of epic battles. Eventually, the gods intervened and declared Horus the rightful king, restoring order and stability to the land.

The story of Ra and Osiris is an essential cornerstone of ancient Egyptian mythology, illustrating the eternal struggle between order and chaos, life and death, and the triumph of good over evil. This timeless tale, filled with adventure, tragedy, and divine intervention, continues to captivate and inspire, offering a glimpse into the rich and complex belief system of one of history's most fascinating civilizations.

# CHAPTER 50: THE MYTH OF ISIS AND OSIRIS: THE AFTERLIFE AND RESURRECTION

The tale of Isis and Osiris is not only an epic story of love and betrayal, but also a narrative that reveals the ancient Egyptians' beliefs about the afterlife and the concept of resurrection. Through their trials and tribulations, Isis and Osiris embodied the cyclical nature of life, death, and rebirth – a concept that was central to Egyptian religion and culture.

As the devoted wife of Osiris and a powerful goddess in her own right, Isis was revered for her incredible resilience and unwavering love. Her tireless efforts to resurrect her husband demonstrated her mastery of magical arts, and her role in the story exemplified the ancient Egyptians' belief in the power of love to transcend even death.

# CHAPTER 51: THE TALE OF HORUS AND SET: THE BATTLE OF GOOD AND EVIL

The epic conflict between Horus and Set is one of the most enthralling and significant stories in Egyptian mythology, representing the eternal struggle between good and evil, order and chaos. This captivating tale offers an insight into the ancient Egyptians' worldview and their understanding of the cosmic balance that governed the universe.

Horus, the falcon-headed god, was the son of Osiris and Isis. He was conceived after the death of his father, who was betrayed and dismembered by his own brother, the malevolent god Set. Set, who represented chaos, disorder, and the harsh desert, usurped the throne of Egypt after murdering Osiris, plunging the kingdom into turmoil and suffering. Horus, who embodied kingship, order, and fertility, was destined to avenge his father's death and reclaim the throne from his wicked uncle.

Raised in secret by his mother, Isis, and the protective goddess Hathor, Horus grew up to become a powerful and skilled warrior. When the time was right, he challenged Set for the throne of Egypt. Their fierce and protracted battle would determine not only the fate of the kingdom, but also the fundamental balance between good and evil in the universe.

The battle between Horus and Set was not a simple duel, but a series of contests and trials that spanned over eighty years. In one of their most famous encounters, the two gods engaged in a boat race, with Horus sailing a boat made of stone and Set navigating a vessel made of heavy, dense wood disguised as stone. Horus's boat, being lighter, easily outpaced Set's, proving his superiority and cunning.

Another critical episode in their struggle occurred when Set managed to blind Horus by gouging out his eyes. However, the resourceful and compassionate goddess Hathor, using the milk of a sacred gazelle, restored Horus's sight, allowing him to continue his quest for justice and retribution.

The ultimate resolution of the battle between Horus and Set came in the form of a divine tribunal, presided over by the gods themselves. After much deliberation and consultation, the gods ultimately sided with Horus, deeming him the rightful ruler of Egypt. Set was defeated, but not entirely vanquished. As a result of the gods' judgment, Horus ascended to the throne, restoring order and harmony to the land.

Despite his defeat, Set was not entirely banished from the pantheon of gods. In an act of reconciliation, he was assigned the role of guarding the celestial boat of Ra, the sun god, as it traversed the dangerous underworld each night. This dualistic nature of Set, embodying both destructive chaos and protective force, is a testament to the ancient Egyptians' understanding of the delicate balance that governed the cosmos.

The tale of Horus and Set is a powerful allegory for the forces of good and evil that shaped the world in the eyes of the ancient Egyptians. Their struggle represents the eternal battle between order and chaos, a conflict that was believed to maintain the balance and harmony of the universe. By examining this captivating story, we can better appreciate the intricate web of beliefs and values that underpinned one of history's most fascinating civilizations.

# CHAPTER 52: THE BOOK OF THE DEAD

The Book of the Dead, also known as "The Book of Coming Forth by Day" or "The Book of Emerging Forth into the Light," is a collection of spells, prayers, and rituals that played a crucial role in ancient Egyptian funerary practices. This fascinating text, which originated during the New Kingdom (circa 1550-1070 BCE) and continued to be used for over a thousand years, guided the souls of the deceased through the treacherous afterlife and helped ensure their eternal well-being.

Each Book of the Dead was uniquely tailored to its owner, containing a selection of spells, prayers, and illustrations that were thought to be most beneficial to the deceased in their journey through the afterlife. The texts were often written on papyrus scrolls, but they could also be found inscribed on tomb walls, coffins, statues, and other funerary objects. Since the Book of the Dead was so important for the deceased's journey in the afterlife, it was often placed within the tomb alongside the mummy and other grave goods.

The spells and prayers in the Book of the Dead encompass a wide range of themes and purposes, including protection from various dangers and supernatural creatures, guidance through the afterlife, provision of food and drink for the deceased, and assistance in overcoming obstacles on the journey to the afterlife. One of the most well-known spells, Spell 125, describes the "Weighing of the Heart" ceremony, a pivotal moment in the deceased's judgment before Osiris, the god of the afterlife.

In the "Weighing of the Heart" ceremony, the heart of the deceased was weighed against the feather of Ma'at, the goddess of truth and justice. This ritual symbolized the evaluation of the deceased's actions and moral character during their life. If the heart was found to be heavier than the feather, it would be devoured by the monstrous Ammit, a fearsome creature with the head of a crocodile, the body of a lion, and the hindquarters of a hippopotamus. This would result in the annihilation of the deceased's soul, condemning them to eternal oblivion.

If, however, the heart was found to be lighter than the feather of Ma'at, the deceased would be declared "true of voice" and allowed to proceed towards the realm of the blessed, known as the Field of Reeds. There, they would enjoy an eternity of bliss, reunited with their loved ones and living in a paradise that resembled their earthly life.

The Book of the Dead also contained vivid and detailed illustrations that complemented the spells and prayers, often depicting the deceased's journey through the afterlife and their encounters with various deities and supernatural beings. These images not only served as visual aids for the spells but also provided a rich source of information about ancient Egyptian beliefs, rituals, and artistic conventions.

The study of the Book of the Dead has shed invaluable light on the religious beliefs and funerary practices of ancient Egypt, revealing a civilization deeply concerned with the fate of the soul in the afterlife. By examining these captivating texts, we can gain a unique insight into the hopes, fears, and aspirations of a people who lived over three thousand years ago, and better understand the enduring appeal of their enigmatic culture.

# CHAPTER 53: ANCIENT EGYPTIAN CONSPIRACIES THE CURSE OF THE PHARAOHS: FACT OR FICTION?

The ancient Egyptians' deep-rooted beliefs in the afterlife and the sanctity of their tombs have given rise to many legends and conspiracy theories, none more famous than the so-called "Curse of the Pharaohs." This alleged curse is said to befall anyone who disturbs the resting place of a pharaoh or other royal personage, bringing misfortune, illness, and even death. But is there any truth behind this chilling tale, or is it merely a product of overactive imaginations and sensationalist media?

The idea of the Curse of the Pharaohs gained widespread notoriety in the early 20th century, following the discovery of King Tutankhamun's tomb by British archaeologist Howard Carter in 1922. The tomb, remarkably well-preserved and filled with priceless treasures, captured the public's imagination and fueled a global fascination with ancient Egypt. However, this discovery was soon overshadowed by a series of mysterious deaths and misfortunes that seemed to befall those connected to the excavation.

The most famous victim of the supposed curse was Lord Carnarvon, the British nobleman who financed the excavation of Tutankhamun's tomb. Just a few months after the tomb's discovery, Carnarvon succumbed to a severe infection resulting from a mosquito bite, sparking rumors that he had been struck down by the curse. As the story spread, it was embellished with eerie details, such as claims that a clay tablet bearing a curse had been found in the tomb, or that a cobra – the symbol of Egyptian royalty – had been spotted in Carter's residence.

While the idea of a vengeful curse makes for a gripping tale, there is little evidence to support its existence. Many of the deaths and misfortunes attributed to the curse can be more plausibly explained by coincidence, natural causes, or even the hazards of early 20th-century archaeology, such as exposure to toxic mold, bacteria, or pesticides used to preserve the artifacts.

Furthermore, the concept of a curse protecting a tomb is not well-documented in ancient Egyptian texts or funerary inscriptions. While some tombs do bear warnings against theft or desecration, these are generally appeals to the gods for justice, rather than threats of supernatural retribution. In fact, the ancient Egyptians believed that a tomb's protective spells and rituals would ensure the deceased's safe passage to the afterlife, making a curse unnecessary.

Despite the lack of concrete evidence for the Curse of the Pharaohs, its enduring popularity can be attributed to several factors. The idea of a mysterious, ancient curse plays into the human fascination with the unknown and the supernatural, while also reflecting a sense of guilt or unease about disturbing the resting places of the dead. Additionally, the story has been perpetuated by sensationalist media coverage and fictional works, which have further blurred the line between fact and fiction.

In conclusion, while the Curse of the Pharaohs makes for an enthralling story, it is more likely a product of myth and speculation than a genuine ancient Egyptian belief or practice. Nonetheless, it serves as a testament to the enduring allure of the ancient Egyptian civilization and the power of its mysteries to captivate our imaginations over three millennia later.

# CHAPTER 54: THE LOST CITY OF ATLANTIS AND ITS CONNECTION TO ANCIENT EGYPT

The story of the lost city of Atlantis has captivated the world for thousands of years, inspiring countless legends, myths, and theories. According to the ancient Greek philosopher Plato, Atlantis was a powerful and advanced civilization that existed around 9,000 years before his time, which would place it in the same era as the earliest stages of ancient Egyptian history. But is there any connection between the two, and could the mysterious Atlantis hold the key to unlocking some of the enigmas of ancient Egypt?

The tale of Atlantis comes to us primarily from Plato's dialogues "Timaeus" and "Critias," in which he describes a great island nation that was located beyond the "Pillars of Hercules" (today's Strait of Gibraltar). This mighty civilization was said to have been founded by the god Poseidon and boasted incredible technological advancements, a highly organized society, and an unparalleled military might. However, after falling out of favor with the gods, Atlantis was allegedly struck by a catastrophic earthquake and tsunami, sinking beneath the waves in a single day and night.

The question of whether Atlantis was a historical reality, a philosophical allegory, or a blend of both has been debated for centuries. Some scholars and researchers have posited that ancient Egypt may hold the key to understanding the true nature of Atlantis, with several theories suggesting a direct connection between the two civilizations.

One such theory proposes that the ancient Egyptians were actually the descendants or survivors of the Atlantean civilization. According to this hypothesis, Atlantean refugees settled in Egypt after the destruction of their homeland, bringing with them their advanced knowledge of science, technology, and spirituality, which helped shape the development of the Egyptian civilization.

Another theory suggests that Atlantis was not a separate civilization but rather a distant colony or outpost of ancient Egypt. This would imply that the Egyptians possessed advanced seafaring capabilities and had established a far-reaching maritime empire, of which Atlantis was a part. Some proponents of this theory point to similarities in the architectural and artistic styles of the two civilizations, as well as the presence of Egyptian artifacts and inscriptions in locations as far afield as the Americas, as evidence of a connection between Egypt and Atlantis.

However, despite the intriguing nature of these theories, there is a lack of concrete evidence to support a direct connection between ancient Egypt and Atlantis. Plato's account of Atlantis is the primary source of information on the subject, and his descriptions are often vague or allegorical, making it difficult to draw definitive conclusions. Furthermore, while there are undeniably some similarities between the two civilizations, these can also be attributed to the widespread influence of ancient Egyptian culture throughout the Mediterranean and Near East.

In conclusion, while the lost city of Atlantis continues to fascinate and inspire, its connection to ancient Egypt remains speculative at best. It is important to approach these theories with a critical eye and a healthy dose of skepticism, as the truth behind the legend may ultimately lie more in the realm of imagination than historical fact. Nonetheless, the enduring appeal of both Atlantis and ancient Egypt serves as a testament to the power of the human spirit and our unquenchable thirst for knowledge about our past and the mysteries it holds.

# CHAPTER 55: THE ALLEGED COVER-UP OF ANCIENT EGYPTIAN ARTIFACTS AND TECHNOLOGY

Throughout history, ancient Egypt has been a source of fascination and mystery. The civilization's advanced knowledge of science, technology, and the arts has led some to believe that there are hidden secrets and suppressed information about the true extent of their achievements. This chapter delves into the alleged cover-up of ancient Egyptian artifacts and technology, exploring the various claims and theories surrounding this controversial topic.

One popular theory revolves around the idea that ancient Egyptian technology was far more advanced than we currently believe, with some even suggesting that they had access to technologies that rival or surpass those of the modern era. Proponents of this theory point to the precision of their architectural feats, such as the Great Pyramids and the Sphinx, as evidence of advanced engineering and construction techniques that have yet to be fully understood or replicated.

Additionally, there are claims that ancient Egyptian artifacts, such as the so-called "Baghdad Battery" and the "Dendera Light," suggest that they had knowledge of electricity and advanced lighting technologies. The Baghdad Battery consists of a clay jar containing a copper cylinder and an iron rod, which some believe was used as a rudimentary galvanic cell, producing an electrical current. The Dendera Light, on the other hand, is a depiction found in the Temple of Hathor at Dendera, which some interpret as an ancient electrical lighting device, possibly a type of Crookes tube or plasma lamp.

Skeptics argue that these interpretations are often based on speculative assumptions and that there are more plausible, conventional explanations for these artifacts. For example, the Baghdad Battery could have been used for electroplating, a technique that was known in antiquity, or simply for storing sacred scrolls. Similarly, the Dendera Light could be a symbolic representation of a mythological or religious concept, rather than a literal depiction of an electrical device.

Another facet of the alleged cover-up involves the notion that certain ancient Egyptian artifacts and discoveries have been deliberately hidden or suppressed by authorities, such as the Egyptian government or international archaeological organizations. Some conspiracy theorists claim that this is done to maintain the status quo and prevent a paradigm shift that could challenge our current understanding of history and human development.

One example often cited by proponents of this theory is the alleged discovery of a secret chamber beneath the Sphinx, which is rumored to contain an ancient library or repository of lost knowledge. Despite numerous investigations and ground-penetrating radar surveys, no such chamber has been conclusively identified, leading some to believe that its existence is being intentionally concealed.

It is essential to approach these claims with caution and a critical mindset, as the evidence supporting them is often tenuous and based on speculation. While it is undeniable that ancient Egypt was a highly advanced civilization, it is also important to remember that our understanding of their culture, knowledge, and technology is continually evolving. New discoveries and advancements in archaeological techniques may yet reveal more about the true extent of their achievements and the secrets that they held.

In conclusion, while the idea of a cover-up of ancient Egyptian artifacts and technology makes for an exciting and intriguing narrative, it is crucial to separate fact from fiction and weigh the evidence carefully. The allure of hidden knowledge and lost secrets is undeniably powerful, but it is essential to approach such claims with a healthy dose of skepticism and critical thinking. By doing so, we can continue to uncover and appreciate the genuine marvels and mysteries of ancient Egypt and their lasting influence on our world.

# CHAPTER 56: EXTRATERRESTRIAL CONNECTIONS: THE BELIEF IN ALIEN CONTACT WITH ANCIENT EGYPTIANS

The mysteries and marvels of ancient Egypt have long captivated the imagination of historians, archaeologists, and enthusiasts alike. Among the myriad of theories and speculations surrounding this enigmatic civilization, one of the most enduring and controversial is the belief that the ancient Egyptians may have had contact with extraterrestrial beings. This chapter delves into the various claims and theories related to this fascinating subject, exploring the possibility of an otherworldly connection between ancient Egypt and beings from beyond our planet.

Proponents of the ancient astronaut theory argue that the advanced knowledge and technological prowess displayed by the ancient Egyptians are evidence of extraterrestrial intervention. They point to the incredible precision and monumental scale of structures such as the Great Pyramids, the Sphinx, and the intricacies of their art, as well as their advanced understanding of mathematics, astronomy, and medicine, as being beyond the capabilities of a civilization that existed thousands of years ago.

One of the most iconic symbols associated with this theory is the Egyptian god Horus, who is often depicted with the head of a falcon. Some ancient astronaut theorists suggest that this representation is actually a depiction of an extraterrestrial being wearing a helmet or other advanced headgear, similar to what modern astronauts might wear. They argue that the gods of ancient Egypt were, in fact, extraterrestrial visitors who shared their knowledge and technology with the Egyptians, helping them to achieve their astonishing feats of engineering and artistry.

Another intriguing aspect of this theory is the idea that ancient Egyptian art and hieroglyphics contain evidence of advanced technology and alien encounters. Proponents point to certain carvings and reliefs that seem to depict unusual or anachronistic objects, such as the "Dendera Light" discussed in a previous chapter, which some interpret as an ancient electrical lighting device. Similarly, the enigmatic "helicopter hieroglyphs" found in the Temple of Seti I at Abydos have been interpreted by some as depictions of modern-day helicopters, submarines, and other advanced vehicles, suggesting a connection to extraterrestrial technology.

Skeptics of the extraterrestrial theory argue that these interpretations are the result of pareidolia, a psychological phenomenon where the human brain perceives familiar patterns or images in random or ambiguous visual stimuli. They maintain that the extraordinary achievements of the ancient Egyptians can be attributed to the ingenuity, determination, and resourcefulness of the people themselves, without the need for intervention from otherworldly beings.

Moreover, experts in Egyptology and archaeology have provided more plausible, conventional explanations for the seemingly enigmatic artifacts and imagery. For example, the "helicopter hieroglyphs" are likely the result of overlapping carvings and erosion over time, creating an illusion of modern vehicles when, in reality, the original inscriptions were more mundane and unrelated to advanced technology.

While the idea of an extraterrestrial connection to ancient Egypt is undoubtedly intriguing, it is crucial to approach such claims with skepticism and critical thinking. By examining the available evidence and considering alternative explanations, we can better understand and appreciate the true nature of this remarkable civilization and its enduring legacy.

In conclusion, the belief in alien contact with ancient Egyptians is a captivating and thought-provoking subject, but it is important to separate fact from fiction and to consider the available evidence critically. The incredible achievements and mysteries of ancient Egypt continue to inspire awe and wonder, and as our knowledge of this enigmatic civilization grows, we may yet uncover more of the secrets that it holds.

## CHAPTER 57: THE CONNECTION TO FREEMASONRY: THE INFLUENCE OF ANCIENT EGYPTIAN SYMBOLS AND ARCHITECTURE ON FREEMASONRY

The Freemasons, a secretive and enigmatic organization with roots in medieval Europe, have long been fascinated by the symbolism, mythology, and architecture of ancient Egypt. The connection between these two seemingly disparate entities is a subject of great interest and speculation, with many Freemasons considering ancient Egyptian knowledge and practices as integral to their craft. This chapter explores the influence of ancient Egyptian symbols, architecture, and culture on Freemasonry, shedding light on the fascinating relationship between these two historical institutions.

One of the most recognizable aspects of Freemasonry is its extensive use of symbols, many of which have origins in ancient Egypt. For example, the Eye of Providence, also known as the All-Seeing Eye, is a symbol commonly associated with Freemasonry and is thought to have been inspired by the Eye of Horus, an important symbol in ancient Egyptian mythology representing protection, power, and good health. Similarly, the square and compass, the most famous symbol of Freemasonry, has been linked to the ancient Egyptian concept of the "stretching of the cord" ritual, used in the foundation of sacred buildings.

The fascination with ancient Egyptian architecture is also evident in the design and layout of Masonic lodges and temples. Masonic lodges often feature elements inspired by Egyptian temples, such as columns, obelisks, and hieroglyphics, as well as more subtle aspects of design, such as proportions and geometry that echo ancient Egyptian principles. Freemasons believe that the knowledge and wisdom of the ancient Egyptian builders, particularly their understanding of sacred geometry, holds the key to unlocking profound spiritual truths and connecting with the divine.

Furthermore, the rituals and ceremonies practiced by Freemasons share similarities with the religious and spiritual practices of ancient Egypt. The initiation rituals of Freemasonry, for example, have been compared to the ancient Egyptian journey through the afterlife, as depicted in the Book of the Dead, with both involving symbolic death and rebirth. Additionally, the use of sacred texts, such as the Egyptian Book of the Dead and the Masonic Book of Constitutions, demonstrates a shared reverence for the written word and its power to transmit knowledge and wisdom.

The allure of ancient Egypt within Freemasonry can be traced back to the organization's early days, with many of its founding members being scholars, antiquarians, and architects who were deeply influenced by Egyptian culture and aesthetics. As Freemasonry grew and evolved, the connection to ancient Egypt was further cemented through the incorporation of Egyptian symbols, rituals, and architectural elements into Masonic tradition.

It is important to note that while the connection between Freemasonry and ancient Egypt is undeniable, it does not imply a direct lineage or influence from the ancient Egyptians to the Freemasons. Instead, the relationship can be seen as one of admiration and inspiration, with the mysteries and wisdom of ancient Egypt providing a fertile ground for the development of Masonic thought and practice.

In conclusion, the influence of ancient Egyptian symbols, architecture, and mythology on Freemasonry is a testament to the enduring power and fascination of this ancient civilization.

The connections between these two historical institutions offer a unique perspective on the transmission and adaptation of ideas across time and culture, enriching our understanding of both ancient Egypt and the enigmatic world of Freemasonry.

# CHAPTER 58: THE HIDDEN CHAMBER OF THE GREAT PYRAMID: THE SEARCH FOR SECRET KNOWLEDGE AND TREASURES

The Great Pyramid of Giza, one of the Seven Wonders of the Ancient World, has long captured the imagination of scholars, explorers, and adventurers, who have sought to uncover its secrets and hidden treasures. The allure of the pyramid is heightened by the tantalizing prospect of undiscovered chambers within its immense structure, which may hold the key to unlocking the mysteries of ancient Egyptian civilization. This chapter delves into the ongoing search for hidden chambers within the Great Pyramid and the potential treasures and knowledge they may contain.

The Great Pyramid was built by Pharaoh Khufu around 2580 BCE as a tomb and monument to his reign. Its construction is an architectural marvel, consisting of over 2.3 million blocks of limestone and granite, some weighing up to 80 tons. While the pyramid's exterior is impressive, it is the interior chambers and passageways that have been the focus of intense exploration and speculation for centuries. The known internal structure consists of the King's Chamber, the Queen's Chamber, and the Grand Gallery, connected by a series of narrow passages. However, it is widely believed that more chambers remain hidden within the pyramid's walls, waiting to be discovered.

The search for hidden chambers within the Great Pyramid has been driven by a combination of historical accounts, architectural analysis, and modern technology. Ancient writings by historians such as Herodotus and Diodorus Siculus described additional chambers and passageways that have yet to be found. Furthermore, the complex design and alignments of the pyramid, as well as the presence of enigmatic features such as the so-called "air shafts," have led many to believe that additional hidden chambers may exist.

In recent years, the search for hidden chambers has been aided by cutting-edge technology, such as ground-penetrating radar, cosmic-ray muon detectors, and 3D imaging. These techniques have enabled researchers to peer into the heart of the pyramid without causing damage to its ancient structure. Several promising discoveries have been made using these methods, including the detection of possible voids or chambers behind the walls of the King's and Queen's chambers, as well as above the Grand Gallery. However, definitive proof and exploration of these potential chambers remain elusive, as gaining access to them poses significant challenges and risks to the pyramid's integrity.

The possibility of finding hidden chambers within the Great Pyramid is more than just an archaeological curiosity; it is also closely tied to the hope of uncovering lost treasures and ancient knowledge. The pyramids were built to house the pharaoh's remains and protect his wealth and possessions for the afterlife. As such, it is believed that the hidden chambers may contain treasures, artifacts, and perhaps even the lost burial chamber of Khufu himself. Additionally, some speculate that the chambers may hold secret knowledge or texts, such as the fabled "Hall of Records," which could reveal profound insights into ancient Egyptian history, culture, and technology.

In conclusion, the search for hidden chambers within the Great Pyramid of Giza is a fascinating and enduring quest, driven by the desire to unlock the secrets of this enigmatic monument. The potential discovery of new chambers, treasures, and knowledge within the pyramid's walls would not only reshape our understanding of ancient Egypt but also add a new chapter to the already rich history of this remarkable civilization. As technology continues to advance and new methods of exploration are developed, the prospects of uncovering the

Great Pyramid's hidden secrets become ever more tantalizing, ensuring that this ancient wonder will continue to captivate the imagination for generations to come.

# CHAPTER 59: THE THEORY OF ANCIENT EGYPTIAN HIGH TECHNOLOGY: THE POSSIBILITY OF ADVANCED TOOLS AND TECHNIQUES USED IN BUILDING THE PYRAMIDS AND OTHER STRUCTURES

The impressive scale and precision of ancient Egyptian architecture, particularly the pyramids, have led to considerable debate and speculation about the methods used in their construction. While mainstream archaeology attributes these feats to the ingenuity and resourcefulness of the ancient Egyptians using simple tools and techniques, alternative theories propose the possibility of advanced tools and technology that may have been employed in building these structures. This chapter delves into the theory of ancient Egyptian high technology and the potential evidence for the use of advanced tools and techniques in their construction.

One of the key arguments for the existence of advanced technology in ancient Egypt is the sheer magnitude and complexity of the structures they built. The Great Pyramid of Giza, for example, consists of over 2.3 million stone blocks, some weighing up to 80 tons, and was constructed with remarkable precision, with its sides aligned to the cardinal points with an accuracy of just a few degrees. Similarly, the temples, obelisks, and statues of ancient Egypt display a level of craftsmanship and detail that is difficult to reconcile with the use of simple tools such as copper chisels, hammers, and wooden levers.

Supporters of the high technology theory point to several intriguing pieces of evidence that suggest the use of advanced tools and techniques in ancient Egyptian construction. For instance, some researchers have identified signs of advanced stone-cutting techniques, such as perfectly straight and smooth cuts in granite and basalt, which would have been extremely difficult to achieve using copper tools. Moreover, the intricate drill holes and circular saw marks found on certain artifacts indicate the use of rotary tools that could cut through hard stone with ease.

Another piece of evidence that supports the theory of advanced technology in ancient Egypt is the existence of the so-called "Baghdad Battery," an artifact discovered in Iraq that dates back to the Parthian period (250 BCE – 224 CE). This artifact consists of a ceramic pot, a copper cylinder, and an iron rod, which some researchers believe functioned as a galvanic cell – a primitive battery. While the Baghdad Battery is not Egyptian, its presence in the region suggests the possibility of ancient knowledge of electricity, which could have been used to power advanced tools and machinery.

The theory of ancient Egyptian high technology also finds support in the writings of various ancient historians and scholars, such as Plato, Herodotus, and Diodorus Siculus, who described advanced techniques and devices used by the Egyptians. For example, Herodotus wrote about the use of "magic words" to move large stones, while Diodorus Siculus mentioned a device called a "tolleno," which could lift and transport heavy objects. While these accounts are often dismissed as exaggerations or misunderstandings, they provide intriguing hints at the possible existence of advanced technology in ancient Egypt.

Skeptics of the high technology theory argue that the evidence for advanced tools and techniques is circumstantial and that the accomplishments of the ancient Egyptians can be adequately explained by their ingenuity and resourcefulness using simple tools and methods. Furthermore, they point out that no direct evidence of advanced technology, such as remnants of machinery or tools, has ever been discovered in Egypt.

The theory of ancient Egyptian high technology presents a fascinating alternative perspective on the construction of the pyramids and other monumental structures. While definitive proof of advanced tools and techniques remains elusive, the tantalizing hints provided by the precision and complexity of these structures, as well as the enigmatic evidence of advanced stone-cutting and possible knowledge of electricity, continue to fuel debate and inspire further research into the mysteries of ancient Egypt. Whether the truth lies in advanced technology or the resourcefulness of a remarkable civilization, thelegacy of ancient Egypt continues to captivate and inspire us today.

As we explore the possibility of advanced technology in ancient Egypt, we must also consider the implications for our understanding of human history and the development of technology. If advanced tools and techniques were indeed used in the construction of the pyramids and other structures, it would suggest that our ancestors possessed knowledge and capabilities that have been lost to time or deliberately concealed. This idea challenges the conventional narrative of human progress and technological development, opening up new avenues of inquiry and speculation.

Moreover, the theory of ancient Egyptian high technology raises questions about the potential influence of external factors on the development of ancient Egyptian civilization. Some proponents of the theory argue that the advanced tools and techniques may have been introduced by visitors from other advanced civilizations or even extraterrestrial beings. While these ideas remain on the fringes of mainstream academia, they underscore the enduring appeal of ancient Egypt as a source of wonder and fascination.

As we continue to study and learn from the achievements of ancient Egypt, it is essential to keep an open mind and consider all possibilities, including the theory of high technology. By doing so, we can deepen our understanding of this extraordinary civilization and its contributions to human history, while also gaining new insights into the potential capabilities of our ancestors.

In this chapter, we have explored the theory of ancient Egyptian high technology, examining the evidence for advanced tools and techniques in the construction of the pyramids and other structures. While the debate continues, and conclusive proof remains elusive, the pursuit of knowledge and understanding of this fascinating civilization is a testament to the enduring allure of ancient Egypt and its mysteries. Whether the ancient Egyptians possessed advanced technology or achieved their feats through sheer ingenuity and perseverance, their legacy remains a powerful reminder of the potential of human achievement and the mysteries that still lie hidden in the sands of time.

# CHAPTER 60: THE DEVELOPMENT OF MATHEMATICS IN ANCIENT EGYPT

The ancient Egyptians made significant contributions to the field of mathematics, developing complex systems for measuring and calculating various quantities. Their advancements in mathematics played a crucial role in their daily life, enabling them to solve practical problems related to agriculture, architecture, commerce, and administration. In this chapter, we will explore the development of mathematics in ancient Egypt, highlighting the key concepts, techniques, and achievements that have left a lasting impact on the history of mathematics.

The Origins of Egyptian Mathematics
The origins of Egyptian mathematics can be traced back to the early dynastic period (c. 3150-2686 BCE), with the earliest known mathematical texts dating to the Old Kingdom (c. 2686-2181 BCE). These early texts primarily focused on solving practical problems related to agriculture, such as calculating land area and the volume of grain storage.

As the Egyptian civilization evolved, the need for more advanced mathematical knowledge grew. The construction of large-scale architectural projects such as the pyramids and temples required precise measurements and calculations. This need for mathematical precision spurred the development of more sophisticated mathematical concepts and techniques.

Numerals and Number Systems
The ancient Egyptians used a base-10 numeral system, which is similar to the decimal system used today. They represented numbers using hieroglyphic symbols, with separate symbols for 1, 10, 100, 1,000, 10,000, 100,000, and 1,000,000. To write

a number, they combined these symbols in a manner similar to our modern notation, making their number system relatively easy to understand and use.

## Arithmetic and Fractions

The ancient Egyptians were skilled in the basic arithmetic operations of addition, subtraction, multiplication, and division. They used a combination of techniques, including doubling and halving, to perform complex calculations.

Egyptian mathematics also made extensive use of fractions. However, they did not use fractions with a numerator greater than one (i.e., they only used unit fractions). To represent other fractions, they would express them as a sum of unit fractions. For example, the fraction 3/4 would be written as 1/2 + 1/4. The Egyptians also used a special symbol called the "eye of Horus" to represent 2/3.

## Geometry and Measurement

Geometry played a vital role in ancient Egyptian mathematics, particularly in the construction of monuments and the calculation of land area for taxation purposes. The Egyptians were familiar with various geometric shapes, such as triangles, rectangles, and circles, and they developed methods to calculate their areas.

One of the most significant contributions of ancient Egyptian mathematics to geometry is the discovery of the Pythagorean theorem, which states that in a right-angled triangle, the square of the length of the hypotenuse is equal to the sum of the squares of the other two sides. Although the theorem is commonly attributed to the Greek mathematician Pythagoras, evidence suggests that the Egyptians knew and applied this theorem several centuries before him.

## Algebra and Problem Solving

Algebra, the branch of mathematics dealing with symbols and the rules for manipulating them, was also a significant part of ancient Egyptian mathematics. Egyptian mathematicians used algebraic methods to solve various types of linear and quadratic equations, often arising from practical problems related to commerce and land measurement.

The ancient Egyptians excelled in problem-solving, using their mathematical skills to tackle real-world challenges. Many Egyptian mathematical texts, such as the Rhind Mathematical Papyrus and the Moscow Mathematical Papyrus, consist of collections of problems and their solutions, demonstrating their prowess in applying mathematics to everyday life.

The development of mathematics in ancient Egypt was a remarkable achievement that laid the foundation for many mathematical concepts and techniques that we still use today. From the basic arithmetic operations and the use of fractions to more advanced concepts in geometry, algebra, and problem-solving, Egyptian mathematicians made significant contributions to the field of mathematics. Their practical approach to mathematics allowed them to address various challenges in agriculture, architecture, commerce, and administration.

These achievements not only showcase the intellectual capabilities of ancient Egyptians but also serve as a testament to the enduring legacy of their civilization. The mathematical knowledge and techniques developed by the Egyptians were eventually passed on to other ancient cultures, such as the Greeks and Romans, contributing to the further development of mathematics throughout history.

Today, as we continue to unravel the mysteries of ancient Egypt, we gain a deeper appreciation for the ingenuity and sophistication of this ancient civilization. The advancements made by Egyptian mathematicians continue to inspire and inform modern mathematical thinking, underscoring the timeless relevance of their work. As we explore the fascinating world of ancient Egyptian mathematics, we are reminded that the pursuit of knowledge and the application of that knowledge to solve practical problems is a defining characteristic of human progress.

# CHAPTER 61: THE INFLUENCE OF ANCIENT EGYPT ON OTHER CIVILIZATIONS

The civilization of ancient Egypt is one of the oldest and most enduring in human history. Over the course of its long history, it left a profound impact on various other civilizations, influencing their culture, politics, religion, and art. This chapter will explore the ways in which ancient Egypt influenced other societies, both in the ancient world and later throughout history.

Mesopotamia: The relationship between ancient Egypt and Mesopotamia was a complex one, characterized by both trade and conflict. As a result, these two civilizations shared ideas and technologies, which in turn influenced their respective cultures. Egyptian art, architecture, and religious practices had a significant impact on Mesopotamian culture. For example, the concept of divine kingship in ancient Egypt inspired Mesopotamian rulers to adopt similar practices, enhancing their own authority and prestige.

The Aegean and Greece: Ancient Egypt's influence on the Aegean world and ancient Greece is well-documented. Greek historians such as Herodotus and Diodorus Siculus were fascinated by Egyptian culture and recorded their observations for future generations. The Greeks adopted various aspects of Egyptian culture, including the use of obelisks, certain architectural styles, and religious practices. The Egyptian practice of mummification also influenced Greek burial customs, while the Greek alphabet was partially inspired by Egyptian hieroglyphics.

The Roman Empire: The conquest of Egypt by Rome in

30 BCE introduced ancient Egyptian culture and art to the Romans, who were captivated by its exoticism and sophistication. Egyptian motifs and themes became popular in Roman art and architecture, and many Roman emperors commissioned Egyptian-style statues and buildings in their own cities. The cult of the Egyptian goddess Isis also gained widespread popularity throughout the Roman Empire, further demonstrating the lasting influence of Egyptian religion.

The Islamic Caliphates: When the Arab Muslims conquered Egypt in the 7th century CE, they were introduced to the rich history and achievements of the ancient Egyptians. This led to a renewed interest in the study of ancient Egyptian culture, history, and sciences. Egyptian knowledge of mathematics, astronomy, and medicine was absorbed by Islamic scholars, who preserved and expanded upon these fields. In turn, this knowledge would later be transmitted to Europe during the Middle Ages, shaping the development of Western science and culture.

The Western World: The rediscovery of ancient Egypt during the Renaissance and the Age of Enlightenment sparked a renewed fascination with its culture, art, and architecture in the Western world. The decipherment of the Rosetta Stone by Jean-François Champollion in the early 19th century led to a deeper understanding of Egyptian history and culture. The study of ancient Egypt has continued to inspire artists, writers, and scholars in the Western world, leading to the development of the field of Egyptology and the preservation of its rich heritage.

In conclusion, ancient Egypt's influence on other civilizations is vast and varied, spanning thousands of years and leaving a lasting impact on various aspects of culture, art, religion, and politics. This influence is still felt today, as the legacy of ancient Egypt continues to captivate and inspire people around the world.

# CHAPTER 62: WARFARE AND MILITARY ORGANIZATION IN ANCIENT EGYPT

Throughout its long history, ancient Egypt experienced periods of both peace and conflict. Warfare played a significant role in the development of the Egyptian state, shaping its borders and influencing its military strategies and organization. This chapter will delve into the intricacies of warfare and military organization in ancient Egypt, examining its evolution over time and the key factors that influenced its development.

Early Egyptian Warfare: In the Predynastic Period, warfare was primarily tribal and local, with conflicts arising over resources such as land and water. Small groups of warriors fought with simple weapons, such as bows, clubs, and spears. The rise of the first pharaohs and the unification of Upper and Lower Egypt in the Early Dynastic Period led to the establishment of a centralized military structure, with a professional standing army and more advanced weaponry.

The Old and Middle Kingdoms: During the Old and Middle Kingdoms, Egypt's military was mainly focused on maintaining internal order and defending its borders from external threats. The Egyptian army was composed of infantry, archers, and charioteers, and was supported by a logistical structure that provided supplies and transport for military campaigns. The construction of forts along the Nile Delta and in Nubia helped to secure Egypt's borders and protect valuable trade routes.

The New Kingdom: The New Kingdom marked a period of territorial expansion and increased military engagement for ancient Egypt. Powerful pharaohs such as Thutmose III, Amenhotep III, and Ramesses II led campaigns into Nubia, Canaan, and Syria, extending Egypt's influence and control over these regions. The Egyptian army became more professional and specialized, incorporating new tactics and technologies such as the horse-drawn chariot and improved weaponry like the composite bow.

Military Organization: The Egyptian military was organized hierarchically, with the pharaoh at the top as the supreme commander, followed by his vizier, who oversaw military administration. Below them were generals who led specific military units, and finally, the soldiers themselves. Soldiers were typically conscripted from the general population and trained in various roles, including infantry, archers, and charioteers. As the military grew in size and complexity, specialized units emerged, such as the Medjay, a group of elite Nubian archers.

The Role of the Navy: The ancient Egyptian navy played a crucial role in both warfare and trade. Naval ships were used for transportation, reconnaissance, and combat during military campaigns. The Nile River and its tributaries provided a natural network for naval transportation, while the Mediterranean and Red Seas allowed Egypt to project its power and influence further afield. The navy also played a significant role in securing trade routes, protecting Egypt's economic interests, and maintaining its status as a regional power.

The Decline of Ancient Egyptian Military Power: In the Late Period, Egypt faced growing threats from external powers such as the Assyrians, Persians, and eventually the Greeks and Romans. The Egyptian military struggled to adapt to new tactics and technologies, and internal strife weakened the state's ability to mount a cohesive defense. Ultimately, Egypt was conquered by foreign powers, bringing an end to its long history as an independent and powerful civilization.

In conclusion, warfare and military organization were integral to the development and maintenance of ancient Egypt as a major power in the ancient world. From the small tribal conflicts of the Predynastic Period to the vast military campaigns of the New Kingdom, the Egyptian military evolved and adapted to the challenges it faced, leaving a lasting legacy on the history and culture of ancient Egypt.

# CHAPTER 63: THE DECLINE OF ANCIENT EGYPT

As we near the end of our journey through the fascinating history of ancient Egypt, it is important to consider the factors that contributed to the decline of this once-great civilization. The fall of ancient Egypt was not an overnight occurrence, but rather a gradual decline that took place over many centuries, marked by periods of internal strife, external invasions, and loss of power. This chapter will explore the reasons behind the decline of ancient Egypt and how it ultimately led to the end of its 3,000-year-old civilization.

Economic Factors: Economic decline played a significant role in the weakening of ancient Egypt. As resources such as gold and valuable trade goods became scarcer, the state's ability to fund large-scale building projects, maintain a strong military, and support the lavish lifestyles of the pharaohs diminished. This decline in wealth also led to an increase in social inequality, which further eroded the stability of the nation.

Political Instability: Political strife was a recurring issue throughout ancient Egyptian history. Dynastic disputes, power struggles, and corruption plagued the government, undermining the authority of the pharaohs and leading to periods of fragmentation and decentralization. During the Third Intermediate Period and Late Period, Egypt was divided into several smaller states, each vying for control and leaving the nation vulnerable to foreign invasion.

Environmental Factors: Climate change and environmental degradation played a role in the decline of ancient Egypt. Long periods of drought, coupled with overuse of agricultural land and deforestation, led to reduced crop yields and food shortages. These issues put further strain on the already weakened economy and contributed to social unrest.

External Threats: Throughout its history, ancient Egypt faced a variety of external threats. The rise of powerful neighboring civilizations, such as the Assyrians, Persians, Greeks, and Romans, presented challenges to Egypt's dominance in the region. As these foreign powers expanded their empires, they increasingly encroached upon Egyptian territory, leading to conflicts and, ultimately, conquest.

Cultural and Religious Changes: The shifting religious and cultural landscape of ancient Egypt also played a part in its decline. The adoption of new religious practices and the spread of foreign cultures diluted the traditional Egyptian beliefs and customs that had once united the people. As the influence of foreign powers grew, the Egyptian people became increasingly divided, further weakening the nation.

The Final Conquests: Despite its gradual decline, ancient Egypt continued to exist as a weakened state until it was finally conquered by a series of foreign powers. First, the Persian Empire under Cambyses II conquered Egypt in 525 BCE, followed by a brief period of independence before it fell to the Greeks under Alexander the Great in 332 BCE. Finally, the Romans annexed Egypt as a province in 30 BCE, effectively ending the ancient Egyptian civilization.

In conclusion, the decline of ancient Egypt was a complex and multifaceted process that spanned centuries. A combination of economic, political, environmental, and cultural factors contributed to the weakening of this once-mighty civilization. Despite its decline, the legacy of ancient Egypt endures, inspiring countless generations with its remarkable achievements in art, architecture, science, and literature. As we reach the end of this historical journey, we are reminded of the resilience and adaptability of the human spirit, as well as the inevitable rise and fall of civilizations throughout time.

# CHAPTER 64: THE SECRETS OF THE SPHINX: DECODING THE MYSTERY

The Great Sphinx of Giza has been shrouded in mystery since its discovery, with historians, archaeologists, and Egyptologists all attempting to unravel its secrets. As one of the world's most iconic and enigmatic monuments, the Sphinx has captured the imagination of countless generations. In this chapter, we delve into the hidden mysteries of the Sphinx and attempt to decode the riddles that surround its creation, purpose, and symbolism.

The Origins of the Sphinx
The Sphinx, a colossal statue of a mythical creature with the body of a lion and the head of a human, is believed to have been built during the reign of the Pharaoh Khafre (c. 2570-2532 BCE) in the Old Kingdom. The monument is located on the Giza Plateau, adjacent to the Great Pyramid of Giza, the final resting place of Khafre himself. The exact purpose of the Sphinx remains uncertain, but many scholars theorize that it served as a guardian to the necropolis, protecting the tombs of the pharaohs.

The Construction and Restoration of the Sphinx
Carved from a single block of limestone, the Sphinx measures 73 meters (240 feet) in length, 20 meters (66 feet) in height, and 14 meters (45 feet) in width. The construction process involved removing the softer layers of limestone to reveal the harder stone beneath, which was then shaped into the iconic form we see today. Over the centuries, the Sphinx has undergone several restoration efforts, most notably in the 14th century CE during the Mamluk period and in the 20th century during modern Egypt's conservation efforts.

Symbolism and Legends

The Sphinx is often considered a symbol of divine protection and wisdom, with its human head representing intelligence and its lion body symbolizing strength. Throughout ancient Egyptian history, the Sphinx was associated with various gods, including Ra, the sun god, and Horus, the god of the sky.

There are also numerous legends and myths surrounding the Sphinx. One of the most famous is the Greek myth of Oedipus and the riddle of the Sphinx. In this tale, the Sphinx poses a riddle to Oedipus, promising to leave the city of Thebes if he can solve it. Oedipus successfully answers the riddle, and the Sphinx throws itself from a cliff in despair.

The Hidden Chambers and the Hall of Records
In recent decades, various theories have emerged about the existence of hidden chambers beneath the Sphinx. Some researchers believe that these chambers may contain the Hall of Records, an ancient library containing invaluable knowledge and artifacts from the lost civilization of Atlantis. While ground-penetrating radar has detected some anomalies beneath the Sphinx, no definitive evidence of hidden chambers or the Hall of Records has been discovered.

The Age of the Sphinx: A Continuing Debate
One of the most enduring debates surrounding the Sphinx is its true age. While the conventional view places its construction during the reign of Khafre, some researchers argue that the Sphinx is much older, possibly predating the dynastic period of ancient Egypt. These theories are based on various factors, such as the erosion patterns on the Sphinx's body, which some believe indicate exposure to heavy rainfall, suggesting an earlier date of construction.

The Great Sphinx of Giza remains a source of fascination and intrigue for historians, archaeologists, and laypeople alike. As we continue to study this enigmatic monument, we may yet uncover more secrets and solve the riddles that have captivated our imaginations for millennia.

# CHAPTER 65: THE GREAT LIBRARY OF ALEXANDRIA: A CENTER OF KNOWLEDGE AND LEARNING

The Great Library of Alexandria, one of the most famous and important libraries of the ancient world, stood as a testament to human knowledge and intellectual curiosity. Housing a vast collection of scrolls and texts, the library was a beacon of learning and a hub of scholarly activity during its time. In this chapter, we explore the history, significance, and legacy of this magnificent institution.

The Founding of the Library
The Library of Alexandria was founded in the third century BCE during the reign of Ptolemy I Soter, a Macedonian general who became the ruler of Egypt after the death of Alexander the Great. Ptolemy's vision for the library was to create a center of learning and knowledge that would rival the great centers of Athens and other Hellenistic cities. His son, Ptolemy II Philadelphus, expanded upon this vision and is often credited with the establishment of the library.

The Collection and Organization of Knowledge
At its height, the Library of Alexandria is estimated to have housed between 400,000 and 700,000 scrolls, containing works on a wide range of subjects, including literature, philosophy, science, history, and mathematics. To facilitate access to this vast collection, the library was organized into different sections, with each section dedicated to a specific subject. The scrolls were cataloged and labeled with tags, allowing scholars to easily find the works they needed.

The Scholars of the Library
The Library of Alexandria attracted the brightest minds of

the ancient world, offering them a place to study, research, and exchange ideas. Among its most famous scholars were Euclid, the father of geometry; Eratosthenes, who calculated the Earth's circumference; and the astronomer and geographer Ptolemy. These scholars and many others contributed to the development of various fields of knowledge and laid the foundation for future scientific advancements.

The Destruction of the Library
The exact circumstances of the Library of Alexandria's destruction remain a subject of debate among historians. It is generally believed that the library suffered multiple incidents of damage and destruction over the centuries, ultimately leading to its complete demise. Some of the most commonly cited events include the fire during Julius Caesar's invasion of Alexandria in 48 BCE, the destruction of the Serapeum by Roman Emperor Theodosius I in 391 CE, and the Arab conquest of Alexandria in 642 CE.

The Legacy of the Library of Alexandria
Despite its tragic end, the Great Library of Alexandria left an indelible mark on human history. The institution's commitment to preserving and advancing knowledge laid the groundwork for the modern concept of libraries and research institutions. Furthermore, the works of the library's scholars have had a lasting impact on various fields of study, including mathematics, astronomy, and geography.

In summary, the Great Library of Alexandria stood as a shining example of the importance of knowledge and intellectual inquiry in ancient Egypt and the wider Hellenistic world. While its destruction marked the end of an era, the legacy of this remarkable institution continues to inspire and inform our pursuit of knowledge today.

# CHAPTER 66: THE TOMB RAIDERS: THE HISTORY AND ETHICS OF ARCHAEOLOGY IN EGYPT

Throughout history, the remarkable tombs and monuments of ancient Egypt have captivated the imagination of explorers, scholars, and tomb raiders alike. The search for hidden treasures and the desire to unlock the secrets of the past led to the development of modern archaeology. However, along the way, this pursuit has raised ethical questions about the treatment of ancient remains and the preservation of cultural heritage. In this chapter, we delve into the history of archaeology in Egypt and examine the ethical considerations surrounding this fascinating field.

Early Exploration and Tomb Raiding
The fascination with ancient Egypt dates back to antiquity, with various Roman emperors known to have collected Egyptian artifacts. However, tomb raiding, which involved the illegal excavation and theft of valuable artifacts from tombs, began during the later periods of ancient Egyptian history. Tomb raiders often caused significant damage to the tombs, destroyed valuable historical information, and dispersed artifacts to private collectors and museums around the world.

The Birth of Modern Archaeology
The 19th century marked a turning point in the exploration of ancient Egypt, as the birth of modern archaeology transformed the study of the past from a pursuit driven by treasure hunting to a more scientific and methodical endeavor. With the arrival of European explorers and the establishment of the Egypt Exploration Society in 1882, the field of Egyptology began to take shape. Pioneering archaeologists such as Auguste Mariette, Flinders Petrie, and Howard Carter made significant discoveries

that deepened our understanding of ancient Egyptian culture and history.

The Preservation and Conservation of Egyptian Heritage
As archaeology in Egypt evolved, so too did the awareness of the need for preservation and conservation. The establishment of the Egyptian Antiquities Service (now the Supreme Council of Antiquities) in the early 20th century marked an important step in the protection and management of Egypt's ancient heritage. The Egyptian government introduced laws to regulate excavations, protect archaeological sites, and ensure that artifacts remained in Egypt for study and display.

The Ethics of Archaeology in Egypt
The history of archaeology in Egypt raises important ethical questions about the treatment of ancient remains, the ownership of cultural heritage, and the responsibilities of archaeologists and institutions involved in the field. Some argue that artifacts should be returned to their country of origin, while others maintain that international museums serve as custodians of global cultural heritage. Additionally, the excavation and display of human remains, such as mummies, bring up ethical concerns about respecting the dead and their cultural beliefs.

The Future of Archaeology in Egypt
As we continue to uncover the secrets of ancient Egypt, the field of archaeology must continue to adapt and address the ethical concerns that arise. International collaboration and dialogue between archaeologists, museums, and governments can help ensure the preservation and respectful treatment of Egypt's ancient heritage, allowing future generations to learn from and appreciate the wonders of this remarkable civilization.

In conclusion, the story of archaeology in Egypt is a complex one, marked by both remarkable discoveries and ethical dilemmas. As we explore the wonders of ancient Egypt in "The

Eternal Sands: A Journey Through Ancient Egypt's Civilization," it is essential to acknowledge the importance of responsible and ethical archaeological practices in preserving and honoring the legacy of this fascinating civilization.

# CHAPTER 67: THE DARK SIDE OF EGYPTIAN MAGIC: CURSES, HEXES, AND BLACK MAGIC

Ancient Egypt is renowned for its remarkable achievements in science, art, and architecture, but it also held a deep fascination with the mystical and the magical. While much of Egyptian magic focused on healing, protection, and ensuring a successful afterlife, there was also a darker side to this practice. In this chapter, we delve into the world of curses, hexes, and black magic in ancient Egypt, uncovering the secrets of these malevolent practices and their role in the lives of the ancient Egyptians.

The Role of Magic in Ancient Egypt

Magic was an integral part of ancient Egyptian society and was believed to permeate all aspects of life. The Egyptians believed that magic, or heka, was a divine force that could be harnessed by priests, magicians, and even ordinary people to manipulate the natural world and influence the gods. While most magic was used for benevolent purposes, such as healing, protection, and ensuring success in the afterlife, there were instances where magic was employed for more sinister ends.

Curses and Protective Spells

Curses were not uncommon in ancient Egypt and were often used as a form of protection against enemies, thieves, and supernatural beings. Tombs, temples, and personal possessions were often inscribed with curses intended to deter would-be intruders or vandals. These curses typically invoked the wrath of the gods, threatening divine punishment on those who violated sacred spaces or stole sacred objects. The most famous example of such a curse is the alleged "Curse of the Pharaohs," which was believed to be responsible for the misfortunes that befell those who disturbed the tomb of Tutankhamun.

## Hexes and Malevolent Magic

While curses were primarily used as a protective measure, hexes were more targeted forms of malevolent magic, intended to cause harm, misfortune, or even death to a specific individual. Ancient Egyptian magicians were believed to be capable of casting powerful hexes by invoking the gods or harnessing the destructive powers of natural elements, such as fire or venomous animals. These hexes were often inscribed on figurines, amulets, or papyri, which were then buried, burned, or submerged in water to activate their power.

## Black Magic and Ancient Egyptian Society

The practice of black magic was generally frowned upon in ancient Egypt, as it was believed to disrupt the natural order and invite chaos and disorder. However, there is evidence to suggest that some individuals sought out the services of black magicians to achieve personal gain or exact revenge on their enemies. The use of black magic was considered a serious offense and could result in severe punishments, such as banishment or even death, for those found guilty of employing it.

## The Legacy of Egyptian Dark Magic

The fascination with the dark side of Egyptian magic persists to this day, fueling popular culture with tales of cursed tombs, sinister sorcerers, and supernatural powers. While the true extent and nature of ancient Egyptian dark magic may never be fully understood, it remains a testament to the complexity and richness of this ancient civilization's spiritual and magical beliefs.

In this chapter, we have explored the darker aspects of ancient Egyptian magic, shedding light on the practice of curses, hexes, and black magic in this fascinating civilization. As we continue our journey through "The Eternal Sands: A Journey Through

Ancient Egypt's Civilization," it is important to remember that the study of ancient Egypt encompasses not only its awe-inspiring achievements but also the more mysterious and enigmatic aspects of its culture and beliefs.

# CHAPTER 68: THE LEGEND OF AKHENATEN: THE HERETIC PHARAOH AND HIS REVOLUTIONARY IDEAS

Akhenaten, one of ancient Egypt's most controversial figures, is often referred to as the "Heretic Pharaoh" due to his radical departure from traditional religious practices. In this chapter, we will delve into the life and reign of Akhenaten, exploring his revolutionary ideas and the lasting impact they had on ancient Egyptian society and culture.

The Early Life of Akhenaten
Born Amenhotep IV, Akhenaten was the son of Pharaoh Amenhotep III and Queen Tiye. He ascended to the throne during the 18th Dynasty, a period marked by unprecedented prosperity and cultural achievements. Initially, Akhenaten followed in the footsteps of his predecessors, worshipping the traditional pantheon of Egyptian gods.

The Rise of Atenism
However, around the fifth year of his reign, Akhenaten underwent a profound religious transformation. He began to elevate the worship of the sun disk, Aten, above all other gods, ultimately declaring Aten as the one true god. This monotheistic shift was a radical departure from the polytheistic beliefs that had dominated ancient Egypt for millennia.

The Construction of Akhetaten
To solidify his new religious doctrine, Akhenaten built a new capital city called Akhetaten, meaning "Horizon of the Aten," in present-day Amarna. This city was dedicated to the worship of Aten and became the center of the new monotheistic religion. Akhenaten also commissioned numerous temples and monuments dedicated to Aten, showcasing a distinctive new

artistic style that celebrated naturalism and the beauty of the sun.

## The Rejection of Traditional Deities

Akhenaten's devotion to Aten came at the expense of traditional Egyptian deities, most notably Amun, the powerful god of Thebes. Akhenaten went so far as to deface and demolish monuments dedicated to Amun, redirecting the resources and wealth previously allocated to his cult to the worship of Aten. This radical shift in religious focus had far-reaching consequences, disrupting the established power structure and causing tension between the pharaoh and the powerful priesthood of Amun.

## The Enigmatic Nefertiti and the Amarna Family

Akhenaten's Great Royal Wife, Nefertiti, played a significant role in his religious revolution. She is often depicted alongside Akhenaten in worship of Aten, and some scholars believe she may have served as a co-regent during his reign. The Amarna family, which included six daughters, was frequently depicted in a naturalistic and intimate style, showcasing the affection and warmth between family members – a stark contrast to the rigid, formal portrayals of previous pharaohs.

## The End of the Amarna Period

Following Akhenaten's death, the Amarna period came to a swift end. His successor, Tutankhamun, restored the worship of the traditional gods and moved the capital back to Thebes. In the years that followed, Akhenaten's name was erased from official records, and his city was abandoned, an attempt to erase his revolutionary ideas from history.

In this chapter, we have explored the fascinating life and reign of Akhenaten, the Heretic Pharaoh. His revolutionary ideas and the dramatic changes he introduced during the Amarna period serve as a testament to the complexity and diversity of ancient Egyptian history. As we continue to delve into the study of this remarkable civilization, we must remember that our understanding of ancient Egypt encompasses both the traditional and the unconventional, painting a rich and multifaceted picture of a culture that continues to captivate us to this day.

# CHAPTER 69: THE ANKH: SYMBOL OF LIFE AND IMMORTALITY

The Ankh, one of the most recognizable symbols of ancient Egypt, is an intriguing emblem that has captivated the minds of historians and enthusiasts alike. This powerful and enduring symbol has a rich history and profound meaning that extends beyond the borders of Egypt. In this chapter, we will explore the origins, significance, and use of the Ankh throughout ancient Egyptian history, as well as its lasting impact on cultures around the world.

Origins and Significance of the Ankh
The Ankh, also known as the "Key of Life" or "Crux Ansata," is a symbol that represents the concept of eternal life, regeneration, and the divine. Its exact origins remain uncertain, but it is believed to have first appeared during the Early Dynastic period (c. 3150 - 2613 BCE). The symbol consists of a cross with a loop at the top, resembling a key. Some theories suggest that the Ankh may represent the union of male and female, or the sun rising over the horizon.

The Ankh in Religion and Ritual
The Ankh was an essential component of ancient Egyptian religious practices and rituals. It was often depicted in the hands of gods and goddesses, signifying their power to grant eternal life to the deceased. In funerary contexts, the Ankh was frequently found in tomb paintings and inscriptions as a symbol of rebirth and the afterlife.

Priests and priestesses would also use the Ankh during religious ceremonies, particularly when invoking the gods or performing blessings. It was believed that the Ankh possessed the ability to transmit divine energy and bestow life upon those it touched.

The Ankh in Art and Architecture
The Ankh was a prevalent symbol in ancient Egyptian art and architecture. It can be found adorning various monuments, temples, and other structures, highlighting its importance within the culture. In many instances, the Ankh was integrated into decorative motifs, such as friezes and hieroglyphics, symbolizing the eternal nature of life and the divine.

The Ankh in Modern Culture
The Ankh has transcended the boundaries of ancient Egypt and become a popular symbol in various cultures worldwide. Today, the Ankh is often found in jewelry, tattoos, and other forms of art, signifying not only its historical and cultural significance but also its enduring appeal as a symbol of life, rebirth, and the divine.

In conclusion, the Ankh is a powerful and enigmatic symbol that has captivated the minds of historians and enthusiasts alike for centuries. Its rich history and profound meaning provide a fascinating glimpse into the complex and diverse world of ancient Egypt, while its enduring appeal in modern culture serves as a testament to the civilization's lasting influence on our understanding of life and immortality.

# CHAPTER 70: THE CREATION MYTH: EXPLORING THE ORIGINS OF THE UNIVERSE

The ancient Egyptians were deeply fascinated by the mysteries of the cosmos and the world's origin. As with many ancient civilizations, they developed creation myths to explain the universe's beginnings, providing a foundation for their religious beliefs and understanding of the world around them. In this chapter, we will delve into the intricacies of the Egyptian creation myths, exploring the different variations and their implications on ancient Egyptian society.

The Heliopolitan Creation Myth
The Heliopolitan creation myth, centered around the city of Heliopolis, was one of the most influential creation stories in ancient Egypt. It revolves around the god Atum, who was believed to have emerged from the primordial waters of chaos called Nun. Atum then created the first divine couple, Shu (air) and Tefnut (moisture), by either spitting them out or through an act of self-procreation.

Shu and Tefnut later gave birth to the sky goddess Nut and the earth god Geb, forming the basis for the Egyptian understanding of the cosmos. Nut and Geb produced four offspring: Osiris, Isis, Seth, and Nephthys. These gods and goddesses played crucial roles in Egyptian mythology, with Osiris representing rebirth and the afterlife, while Seth embodied chaos and destruction.

The Memphite Creation Myth
The Memphite creation myth originated in the city of Memphis, where the god Ptah was considered the supreme creator deity. This myth focuses on the power of words, asserting that Ptah

created the universe through his thoughts and speech. He first conceived the world in his mind, then brought it into existence by reciting divine words.

The Memphite myth emphasizes the significance of language and the spoken word in ancient Egyptian society. It also highlights the importance of Memphis as a center of religious and intellectual thought during the Old Kingdom.

### The Hermopolitan Creation Myth

The Hermopolitan creation myth, associated with the city of Hermopolis, is centered around the Ogdoad, a group of eight primordial gods and goddesses. These deities were represented as pairs of male and female gods, each embodying a specific aspect of the chaotic waters from which the universe emerged. The Ogdoad consisted of Nu and Naunet (water), Huh and Hauhet (infinity), Kek and Kauket (darkness), and Amun and Amaunet (hiddenness).

According to the Hermopolitan myth, the Ogdoad combined their powers to create a mound of earth from the chaos, upon which the sun god emerged and brought light to the world. This story emphasizes the significance of balance and duality in Egyptian cosmology.

### The Theban Creation Myth

The Theban creation myth was centered around the city of Thebes and the god Amun-Ra. This story combines elements from both the Heliopolitan and Hermopolitan myths, presenting Amun-Ra as the ultimate creator deity who emerged from the primordial waters of Nun. Amun-Ra then created the world and other gods through the power of his divine words, similar to Ptah in the Memphite myth.

As with the other creation stories, the Theban myth underlines the importance of Thebes as a religious and political center during the New Kingdom period.

In conclusion, the various Egyptian creation myths reveal a complex and nuanced understanding of the cosmos and its origins. These myths not only provided a framework for ancient Egyptian religious beliefs but also offered insights into the culture and values of this remarkable civilization. The creation stories continue to captivate and inspire, offering a glimpse into the eternal sands of a civilization that has fascinated generations of scholars and enthusiasts alike.

# CHAPTER 71: THE EGYPTIAN PANTHEON: LESSER-KNOWN GODS AND THEIR STORIES

While the main gods and goddesses of ancient Egypt, such as Osiris, Isis, Ra, and Horus, are widely recognized and celebrated, the Egyptian pantheon is vast and includes numerous lesser-known deities. These gods and goddesses played various roles in the lives of the ancient Egyptians, offering protection, guidance, and support in different aspects of life. In this chapter, we will explore some of these lesser-known gods and their stories, shedding light on their significance in ancient Egyptian religion and society.

Bes: The Protector of Households and Women in Labor
Bes was a unique god in the Egyptian pantheon, often depicted as a dwarf with a lion-like face, a beard, and large, protruding ears. He was a protector of households, particularly women and children, and was known to ward off evil spirits and misfortune. Bes was also associated with music, dance, and merriment. Amulets and statuettes of Bes were common in ancient Egyptian homes, and he was often depicted on the walls of temples and tombs.

Taweret: The Hippopotamus Goddess of Childbirth and Fertility
Taweret was a goddess with the body of a hippopotamus, the limbs of a lion, and the tail of a crocodile. She was a protective deity of childbirth and fertility, and pregnant women often wore amulets depicting Taweret to ensure a safe pregnancy and delivery. The ancient Egyptians believed that Taweret protected women and their unborn children from evil spirits and malevolent forces, making her a vital figure in Egyptian households.

Khnum: The Ram-Headed Creator God
Khnum was an ancient Egyptian god with the head of a ram
who was associated with the source of the Nile River. He was
considered a creator god, responsible for crafting human beings
and their souls on his potter's wheel. Khnum was also believed
to have created the other gods and goddesses, the heavens, and
the Earth itself. His cult center was located on the Island of
Elephantine, near Aswan, where the annual flooding of the Nile
began.

Wepwawet: The Jackal God of Warfare and Hunting
Wepwawet was a jackal-headed god who was often associated
with Anubis. However, while Anubis was primarily associated
with the afterlife and mummification, Wepwawet's role was
centered around warfare, hunting, and the opening of the way.
He was considered a guardian and guide, leading the pharaoh
and his army to victory in battle. Wepwawet's primary cult
center was the ancient city of Asyut in Upper Egypt.

Heka: The God of Magic and Medicine
Heka was the personification of magic and medicine in
ancient Egypt. He was believed to have been present at the
creation of the world and wielded great power over the forces
of nature. Heka was often depicted carrying a staff with two
intertwined snakes, which later became the symbol of the
medical profession. The ancient Egyptians believed that Heka's
power could be harnessed through rituals, spells, and amulets,
allowing them to influence the world around them.

These lesser-known gods and goddesses reveal the depth
and complexity of the ancient Egyptian pantheon. They
played vital roles in the daily lives of the Egyptians, providing
protection, guidance, and support in various aspects of life. By
understanding the stories and significance of these deities, we
gain a more comprehensive understanding of the rich tapestry
of ancient Egyptian religion and the beliefs that shaped this

remarkable civilization.

# CHAPTER 72: THE TREASURES OF THE CAIRO MUSEUM: A GLIMPSE INTO ANCIENT EGYPT'S ARTISTIC HERITAGE

The Cairo Museum, officially known as the Egyptian Museum, is home to one of the world's most extensive collections of ancient Egyptian artifacts. Located in Cairo, Egypt's bustling capital, the museum showcases the rich artistic heritage of this fascinating civilization, offering a unique window into the lives, beliefs, and artistic talents of the ancient Egyptians. In this chapter, we will explore some of the most remarkable treasures housed within the Cairo Museum and learn about their significance in understanding ancient Egypt's artistic and cultural legacy.

The Gold Mask of Tutankhamun
Perhaps the most famous artifact in the Cairo Museum is the gold mask of Tutankhamun, a young pharaoh who ruled Egypt during the 18th Dynasty. Discovered in 1922 by British archaeologist Howard Carter, the mask is made of solid gold and adorned with precious stones, including lapis lazuli, turquoise, and carnelian. The mask is a prime example of the exquisite craftsmanship and artistic skill of ancient Egyptian artisans, and its discovery helped to spark a renewed interest in Egyptology worldwide.

The Narmer Palette
The Narmer Palette, dating back to the Early Dynastic Period (circa 3100 BCE), is a significant artifact in the study of ancient Egyptian history. The palette, made of green schist, features detailed carvings that depict King Narmer, who is believed to have united Upper and Lower Egypt. The scenes on the palette showcase Narmer wearing the crowns of both regions, symbolizing the unification of the two lands under his rule. The Narmer Palette is a vital historical artifact that provides insight

into the origins of the ancient Egyptian state.

The Statue of Khafre
The Statue of Khafre is a magnificent example of ancient Egyptian sculpture. Khafre was a pharaoh of the Fourth Dynasty, who is also known for commissioning the construction of the second-largest pyramid at Giza. The statue, made of diorite, depicts the seated pharaoh wearing a royal headdress, known as the nemes, with a falcon symbolizing the god Horus embracing him from behind. The statue's intricate details and lifelike features showcase the remarkable skill and talent of ancient Egyptian sculptors.

The Rosetta Stone
While the original Rosetta Stone is housed in the British Museum in London, a replica can be found in the Cairo Museum. The Rosetta Stone, discovered in 1799, is inscribed with a decree issued by King Ptolemy V in 196 BCE. The text is written in three scripts: hieroglyphics, Demotic, and Greek, which enabled scholars to decipher the long-lost hieroglyphic script and unlock the secrets of ancient Egyptian history and culture.

The Collection of Amarna Art
The Amarna Period, during the reign of the "heretic" pharaoh Akhenaten, marked a significant departure from traditional Egyptian artistic styles. The Cairo Museum houses an extensive collection of Amarna art, characterized by more naturalistic and expressive representations of people, animals, and plants. These artifacts provide insight into the religious and cultural upheaval that occurred during Akhenaten's reign, as he attempted to replace the traditional polytheistic religion with the worship of a single god, the sun disk Aten.

These treasures, along with countless other artifacts, make the Cairo Museum an essential destination for anyone interested in ancient Egyptian history, art, and culture. The museum's vast collection offers a glimpse into the artistic heritage of this captivating civilization, revealing the depth and complexity of their beliefs, rituals, and creative expressions. By studying these artifacts, we can better understand and appreciate the incredible legacy left behind by the ancient Egyptians, and the profound impact they had on the development of human civilization.

## The Fayum Mummy Portraits

The Fayum mummy portraits are a unique collection of encaustic paintings on wooden panels that were placed over the faces of mummified bodies. These portraits, dating back to the Roman Period in Egypt (1st to 3rd centuries CE), provide a rare glimpse into the faces of ancient Egyptians who lived during this time. The portraits display a range of artistic styles, from realistic to more stylized representations, and reflect the fusion of Egyptian, Roman, and Greek artistic traditions.

## The Statue of Ramses II

Ramses II, also known as Ramses the Great, was one of the most powerful and celebrated pharaohs of ancient Egypt. The Cairo Museum houses a colossal statue of Ramses II, which once stood at the entrance of the Ramesseum, his mortuary temple. The statue, made of red granite, stands over 10 meters (33 feet) tall and weighs around 83 tons. It exemplifies the grandeur and power associated with Ramses II and his reign.

## The Collection of Papyrus Manuscripts

The Cairo Museum also holds an extensive collection of papyrus manuscripts that cover various aspects of ancient Egyptian life, from religious texts and spells to administrative records and literary works. These papyri provide invaluable information on ancient Egyptian language, religion, culture, and daily life, further enriching our understanding of this fascinating civilization.

## The Statues of Hatshepsut

Hatshepsut was a rare female pharaoh who ruled Egypt during

the 18th Dynasty. The Cairo Museum houses a collection of statues depicting Hatshepsut, which were discovered at her mortuary temple in Deir el-Bahari. These statues display the pharaoh in both feminine and masculine attire, reflecting her unique position as a female ruler in a male-dominated society.

The Royal Mummy Rooms
The Cairo Museum's Royal Mummy Rooms contain the mummified remains of several prominent pharaohs and queens, including Ramses II, Seti I, Amenhotep III, and Queen Hatshepsut. These mummies provide a direct connection to the individuals who shaped ancient Egypt's history, and their study has offered significant insights into ancient Egyptian mummification practices, health, and lifespans.

The Cairo Museum's vast collection of artifacts and treasures offers visitors an unparalleled opportunity to delve into the rich history and artistic heritage of ancient Egypt. Each artifact, from monumental statues to delicate jewelry, tells a story that adds to our understanding of this extraordinary civilization. By examining these treasures, we continue to learn more about the lives, beliefs, and accomplishments of the ancient Egyptians, ensuring that their legacy endures through the ages.

# CHAPTER 73 : A TIMELESS JOURNEY THROUGH THE SANDS OF ANCIENT EGYPT

As we reach the end of this extraordinary journey through the pages of "The Eternal Sands: A Journey Through Ancient Egypt's Civilization," it is time to pause and reflect on the incredible legacy of a civilization that has captivated the world for millennia. From the earliest days of the Nile Valley's first settlements to the rise and fall of its great pharaohs, we have explored the fascinating history, culture, and achievements of ancient Egypt.

In our travels, we have uncovered the mysteries of the pyramids, the secrets of the mummification process, and the awe-inspiring tales of gods and goddesses. We have delved into the world of art, literature, and science, examining the innovations that continue to influence modern society. Through stories of powerful female rulers and everyday life, we have gained a deeper understanding of the role of women in ancient Egyptian society. We have also ventured into the realm of ancient Egyptian myths, legends, and conspiracies, sparking our imagination and fueling our curiosity.

Throughout this book, we have strived to provide a comprehensive and engaging account of ancient Egypt, illuminating both its remarkable achievements and its enduring mysteries. It is our hope that the journey has been as captivating for you, the reader, as it has been for us. We are grateful for your companionship on this adventure and thank you for allowing us to share our passion for ancient Egypt with you.

As we close the final chapter of "The Eternal Sands," let us take a moment to appreciate the beauty and wonder of ancient Egypt.

The civilization's majestic monuments stand as a testament to human ingenuity and the power of the human spirit. Their resilience in the face of time, the elements, and countless invasions speaks to the indomitable nature of the culture and the people who built it.

The legacy of ancient Egypt endures not only in the physical remnants of its once-great civilization but also in the stories, ideas, and knowledge that have been passed down through the generations. The wisdom of ancient Egypt continues to resonate today, offering insights into the human experience and inspiring us to learn more about the past.

In the end, the sands of time may have obscured some of the details of ancient Egypt's history, but the essence of its civilization remains eternal. The echoes of its past continue to captivate us, drawing us in and inviting us to explore further. As we bid farewell to the land of the pharaohs, let us carry with us the sense of wonder and curiosity that has fueled our journey through the pages of "The Eternal Sands." May our newfound knowledge and appreciation for ancient Egypt inspire us to continue exploring the rich tapestry of human history, ever mindful of the lessons and beauty that lie hidden within the eternal sands.

Thank you, dear reader, for accompanying us on this unforgettable adventure through the annals of ancient Egypt. As we part ways, we leave you with the hope that the spirit of this remarkable civilization will continue to inspire and captivate your imagination for years to come.

[1]

# BOOKS BY THIS AUTHOR

**The Ever-Changing Tapestry: A Journey Through The History Of Britain**

**The Crown Through The Ages: A History Of The British Monarchy**

**Quantum Realities: Uncovering The Mysteries Of The Universe And The Multiverse**